Rehabilitation of Partially Di

An International Perspective

Rehabilitation of Partially Disabled People

An International Perspective

Editors

Saskia Klosse
Stella den Uijl
Tineke Bahlmann
Joop Schippers

THESIS PUBLISHERS
AMSTERDAM 1998

ISBN 90-5170-439-9
NUGI 695/681

Layout/editing: G.J. Wiarda Institute, Utrecht University Institute for Legal Studies
Cover design: Mirjam Bode
AWSB-logo cover: BRS Premsela Vonk

Table of Contents

TABLE OF CONTENTS

VI

Rehabilitation of Partially Disabled People: Achievable on What Conditions?

Stella den Uijl, Saskia Klosse, Tineke Bahlmann and *Joop Schippers*

1 Theme

Compared to its neighbouring countries the Netherlands have a relatively large number of people who receive income support under the various Sickness and Disability Insurance Acts. Because of the enormous costs involved, a considerable number of measures have been taken with a view to reducing this large number of people who live on benefits in stead of on wages.

Although these measures are fairly diverse, it is possible to make a broad distinction between two types of measures. Roughly speaking, there are measures which primarily aim at producing a reduction in the expenditures on benefits, and there are measures which are intended to bring about reintegration of beneficiaries in the workforce.[1]

Examples of measures falling within the first category are various sorts of cost reducing measures, such as lowering the rate of benefits, restricting the duration of benefits and/or imposing stricter eligibility conditions for benefits.

A striking example of the second type of measure can be found in the Employment of Handicapped Workers Act (in Dutch: *Wet Arbeid Gehandicapte Werknemers, WAGW*), which came into force in 1986. This Act compels employers (organizations) and trade unions to create, in as far as this is reasonably possible, equal opportunities for disabled and able-bodied people with respect to participation in employment. Statistics show nevertheless, that in spite of all this the rehabilitation or reintegration of partially disabled people in the workforce still proceeds very slowly.

Over the last few years the problem of insufficient reintegration of partially disabled people has become an issue of growing political concern. The increasing awareness of the great importance of having as many as possible people participate in the labour process, plays a significant role. Sprouting from this awareness, the promotion of reintegration of partially disabled people was given highest priority during the Nineties. In order to achieve this goal, this time emphasis was put on strengthening the sense of individual responsibility of employers and employees to cooperate in ensuring the financial feasibility of the social security system. Active reintegration policy at company level seems an effective way to meet this responsibility.

1

Promoting the rehabilitation of partially disabled people is not a typically Dutch issue. Other countries too have put this problem on the political agenda. This is the case in Norway and Sweden as well as in neighbouring countries such as Germany and the United Kingdom.

There are, of course, a number of significant historically based differences between the structure and organization of the social security systems of these countries. However, that does not mean that rehabilitation as a functional process is not quite similar in all of these countries. The position of partially disabled people is in principle the same everywhere and usually rehabilitation has to be brought about via cooperation of the same actors. Thus, the ways in and the means by which this reintegration is achieved do not differ as much as they would seem to at first sight.

This actually also holds for the reason behind taking reintegration stimulating measures. Not only the Netherlands but other countries too are aware of the importance of such measures, if only to reshape the social security system so that it may once again meet its original goal, namely guaranteeing only a temporary compensation for loss of income (Elshoff, 1995). Apart from Germany where this notion was translated into the rule of thumb that 'Rehabilitation geht vor Rente' ('Rehabilitation before compensation') already in the early Sixties, this is also apparent in, for example, the Scandinavian principle of 'work-line' which, like the aforementioned German rule, gives priority to reintegration.

In view of these similarities it seems interesting enough to take a closer look at the measures taken and instruments used in other countries to reintegrate partially disabled people. Studying the methods used in those other countries may, after all, contribute to a better understanding of the factors that may hinder such reintegration or, rather, help to reach that goal.

It is against this background that the present book was compiled.

In order to increase our understanding of the factors that can contribute to successful reintegration of partially disabled people into the workforce, experts from various European countries have been invited to write a contribution for this book. These experts come from Sweden, Norway, Germany, Belgium and the United Kingdom, as well as from the Netherlands.

The choice of these countries is not arbitrary; they were chosen on the basis of a number of standard options that can be distinguished in the field of reintegration stimulation. These standard options in turn can be found by analysing what policy choices were made as regards the distribution of responsibility for the achievement of reintegration of partially disabled people. A number of basic choices seems to be available in this respect. Studying the systems used in the abovementioned countries we learn that the actual choice is mostly determined by the question whether the responsibility for successful reintegration lies primarily with the government, or with (the organizations of) employers and employees and/or the partially disabled themselves.

From the various contributions in this book it will be clear that there is no single answer possible to this question. In reality the matter of responsibility allocation proves to be one of many nuances and variations. Most countries do not allocate sole responsibility to either of these three parties. Rather, there appear to be various mixed arrangements.

Although the above seems to indicate that allocation of responsibility for successful reintegration is rather a matter of 'more or less' than of 'either or', it is nevertheless possible to discern certain basic options which are at the roots of the various mixed varieties.

Thus, in Scandinavian countries the responsibility for reintegration enhancement is primarily a government matter. It is only during the 90s that this changes in that since then the so-called work-line policy entered the scene (alongside government responsibility). This choice entails a stricter individual responsibility for employers to employ (and keep employed) partially disabled people.

In other countries, such as Germany and the UK, the earlier introduction of a quota system already expressed the option in this field to apportion clear individual responsibility to employers. After all, this system obliges employers to hire a certain percentage of partially disabled people.

Aside from the fact that in the UK this system has already been abandonned, the Netherlands and Belgium have not opted for such directly coercive measures. In these countries too it is acknowledged that the basic responsibility is shared with employers (and partially disabled themselves) but this responsibility has not been delineated further by introducing direct legally enforceable obligations. Especially in the Netherlands we can discern these last few years an inclination to change the situation. Again, however, this is not done by making the responsibility of employers (and partially disabled employees) more obvious by introducing directly coercive measures. Rather, positive and negative stimuli will have to induce employers to make their contribution to the realization of the reintegration goal. In essence this implies the option to shape the employers' responsiblity in reintegration promotion indirectly. Besides, government institutions will also have to chip in. This indicates, therefore, rather more of a shared responsibility allocation as we see in the Scandinavian countries.

As we assume that the abovementioned indicated basic options for responsibility allocation as regards realization of reintegration will, via the related choice for specific instruments, have their influence on the extent in which the reintegration goal is achieved, we will analyse the factors that may contribute positively or negatively to this process from this point of view.

2 Added Value of the Book

Based on descriptive research (Nijhuis, 1995) a large number of elements that are related to reintegration are mentioned in literature. We can distinguish factors that enhance reintegration with the former employer or with a new employer.

Factors that may play a positive role in reintegration with the former employer encompass:
- large scale company;
- high degree of satisfaction of the employer with the functioning of the now partially disabled worker;
- close contact with the partially disabled worker;
- long employment contract;
- high average age of partially disabled worker;
- possibilities for function adaptation;
- possibilities for adaptation of employment contract.

As regards reintegration with a new employer, the following factors may contribute positively:
- smaller scale company;
- more active search actions on the part of the partially disabled;
- lower average age;
- further possibilities for the organization to employ people on temporary contracts.

More general factors that may have a positive influence on reintegration both with old and new employers are improved health of partially disabled people, higher sense of personal employability and stronger focus of the partially disabled employee on work. However, the labour market situation in a country or region, and the financial economic position of a company are also factors that affect reintegration of partially disabled people in the labour process.

From a point of view of practical policy recommendations these descriptive researches are often disillussions. They provide little information on the interaction

4

of factors that lead to successful reintegration of partially disabled people in the labour process or on the way in which this can be enhanced. It therefore seems important to further investigate the demands which systematic reintegration policies ought to meet. This collection intends to contribute by critically analyzing the different methods for reintegration enhancement as applied in the various countries. Ultimate goal is to thus obtain a better understanding of the basic demands a reintegration policy has to meet in order to achieve successful reintegration.

3 Structure of the Book

In order to find an answer to the question what factors will have a positive effect on the reintegration process, this collection opens with a contribution outlining the current state of affairs as regards the Dutch social security system. According to Den Uijl and others two main tendencies can be discerned.

On the one hand there is a shift from a collective solidarity system towards a selective market-orientated model. Increased market-orientation and selectiveness are to reduce the number of new claimants under disability schemes. This shift in emphasis is motivated mainly by financial reasons. At the same time the solidarity principle loses significance.

On the other hand the number of disability scheme beneficiaries leaving the system must be increased by means of reintegration instruments. Another problem involved is that within labour organizations there is an ever increasing pressure to raise productivity levels. That development is hard to reconcile with the aim of hiring and/or keeping (more) partially disabled employees. After all, it is especially this group of workers that is supposed to be unable to meet higher productivity demands. Realization of that reintegration goal is thus hampered.

This negative effect is strengthened further as the solidarity principle is less and less important due to the shift towards a selective market-orientated social security system. Reintegration of partially disabled people, after all, requires solidarity of the employers with partially disabled people. Whether, and if, in how far more market-orientation and selectiveness actually contribute to realization of reintegration is thus at least dubious. Whether, and if, to what extent this is the case will be reviewed in chapter 1.

In chapter 2 Westerhäll reviews the Swedish situation. It becomes clear that the shortage of labour during the Eighties was actually the motor behind the reintegration promoting measures taken during the Nineties. However, by the time these took effect labour market circumstances had changed drastically. The labour market of the

early Nineties was characterized by a severe economic depression, high unemployment and a changed market structure. Reintegration under such circumstances is hard
to realize, as we learn from the Swedish contribution.

Apart from the changed market situation other factors too prove to have been at the
root of the problems. Thus, the Swedish 'work-line' policy is to a large degree
hampered by the fact that the employer's responsibility is defined in insufficiently
clear terms. As a result various interpretations are possible of when the employer has
met his obligations. This in turn causes disputes about the scope of the employer's
responsibility and what means he must apply.

Further unclarity exists about the distribution of responsibilities between employers
and the government institutions involved with reintegration.

The problems this causes are increased by the various government institutions
responsible for reintegration all having their own different views on what needs to
be done and what not in order to promote reintegration. Each institution in principle
has its own aim which in practice easily results in conflicting priorities with all the
obvious consequences. One of them being that the partially disabled worker gets
caught inbetween and that in the end reintegration fails to be achieved.

Despite all these problems Westerhäll sees no reason to fundamentally change the
system. Some improvements are necessary though in order to remove as many
obstacles as possible. Further specification of the employers' responsibilities in
legislation seems crucial in this context. This can be done, e.g., by formulating clear
criteria that have to be met by the employer and by introducing sanctions in case of
failure to comply. Alongside these measures or in addition thereto financial stimuli
can be considered such as an employer period, during which the employer
temporarily has to pay sick-benefit to employees who are unable to work due to
sickness. Apart from this sort of measures which influence employer behaviour, it
seems furthermore necessary to take measures aiming at improving coordination
between the various government institutions responsible for reintegration promotion.

In chapter 3 Kjønstad pictures the Norwegian situation in the field of reintegration.
In Norway primary responsibility for the welfare of (partially) disabled people lies
with the government. Individual citizens and labour organizations have a limited
statutory responsibility in this regard. Although in Norway too partially disabled
people have fewer chances at participation in the labour process, there is no quota
system as in Germany nor are their chances improved via anti-discrimination
legislation as happens in Anglo-American countries. There are possibilities to grant
employers wage cost subsidies in order to stimulate the hiring of partially disabled
employees. Nevertheless, this instrument has not prevented many employers to

gradually begin using the (luxurious) social security system as a means to 'dump' surplus personnel.

In order to stem this tide, certain changes were introduced in the social security system in the Nineties. These changes mostly concern a reduction of benefits claims in case of longterm disability. The aim was in the first place to achieve a reduction in costs. At the same time, however, the 'work-line' policy was introduced in Norway too, aiming to contribute to promoting (actual) participation of partially disabled people in the labour process. Kjønstad in his contribution doubts whether the way in which this was structured was sufficient. These doubts are confirmed by the fact that the supposed necessity to curb costs is one of the reasons behind introducing the 'work-line' policy. Irrespective of whether this will lead to successful lasting reintegration, Kjønstad fears that this approach will in the end (only) result in undermining the ideology of humanity and solidarity, which is at the basis of the entire system of social security. Ergo, in stead of to social security this leads to increased social insecurity, with all attendant consequences.

Chapter 4 presents Winkler's view on the current German situation. Here we learn that though the German quota system is a necessary condition, it certainly is not a sufficient condition to create equal opportunities for partially disabled people in the labour market. In practice the obligation for employers to hire a certain percentage of partially disabled employees, which stems from this system, proves to induce employers to evasive behaviour. The statutory system offers the possibility to buy off the quota obligation by paying a levy and this is widely used. Besides, this system also proves to bring employers to apply risk selection. And so it is clear that direct coercion instead of stimuli can prove an important obstruction to actual reintegration. In order to counter this averse effect, Winkler considers additional measures necessary. He has especially measures in mind concerning counselling as well as giving out information on reintegration promoting measures. From the conviction that an important obstacle for realizing reintegration is the negative image employers have of the remaining labour possibilities of partially disabled people, he emphasizes the importance of measures that help reduce the possible risks and insecurities related to hiring these people. In this context he advocates a better use of the possibility to temporarily hire people via employment agencies. Thus, employers can find out in practice what partially disabled people are capable of. Once they have been convinced they will much sooner take the chance and employ partially disabled employees on a longterm basis.

Samoy reviews in chapter 5 the reintegration of partially disabled people as regards developments in the labour market in Belgium. In doing so he draws attention to the fact that for most partially disabled their handicap is not the only and sometimes not even the most important 'personal factor' which causes their problems in the labour market. The position of a certain group in the labour market depends on the attitude and behaviour of members of that group, of potential employers and probably also of employment organizations. The relevance of personal factors such as age, gender, education, race and health and also how these are perceived by all parties involved, determine the attitude of those parties. Employers assess the health factor in a cost-benefit analysis. They assess a partially disabled person not only as regards the fact whether he is technically capable of doing the job. Stereotype perceptions of what partially disabled people can or cannot do also play an important role in the selection.

Samoy points in this context to the problem that those segments of the labour market where others with weak labour market positions present themselves are also the segments where the partially disabled have to resort to. As a result partially disabled people usually face the same problems when trying to return to the labour market as other problem groups, such as unskilled longterm unemployed and older unemployed people; they often have the same characteristics and are thus faced with the same obstacles on their way back to the labour market. It is in this respect that Samoy wonders whether specific reintegration policies for the various groups are desirable or indeed necessary. Such policies after all entail the introduction of different sorts of legislation and different sorts of (government) institutions with individual, differing goals and competences. In short, such policies lead to a completely fragmented system with all the inherent dangers of overlap and inefficiency. It will be obvious that the realization of reintegration is then frustrated rather than enhanced. In order to improve the situation Samoy pleads for an integrated reintegration policy, where the skills and expertise of professionals are combined. This should leave sufficient room to pay attention to the specific problems partially disabled people face when returning to the labour process. The client friendlyness of the system, in other words, should not disappear. What has to be taken care of though is that reintegration policy is less segregated than is now the case.

In chapter 6 Thornton and Lunt discuss the situation in the United Kingdom. It appears that in the United Kingdom one can discern a tendency from promoting reintegration of partially disabled as a group towards a more individual reintegration policy. The government withdraws its responsibility in this regard and in stead places the emphasis on creating conditions which must enhance the individual chances of partially disabled people in the labour market. More concrete this has been done by introducing an anti-discrimination act. This act must help particularly the partially disabled unemployed in fighting the competition in the labour market.

Opting for this measure entails a policy change in the sense that employers are no longer obliged via a quota regulation to employ partially disabled people. From now on they will be pushed to do so by the anti-discrimination act. The responsibility for the success of reintegration is thus placed with the market parties, that is to say, with the employers (organizations and fora) on the one hand and with the individual partially disabled employee on the other.

However, the authors doubt whether this will prove sufficient. To support their argument they point out the fact that this system in itself contains very few stimuli to entice employers to hiring partially disabled workers. A possibility to change this is to 'damage' the image of the employer (and his profits) who hires no or hardly any partially disabled people, by branding him a bad employer. He is thus blackened as compared to the good employers who do employ partially disabled people. Whether this would have the intended result is doubted by Thorton and Lunt, because the good employers who may put this in their advertisements, already contributed to reintegration promotion. And that bad employers will change tactics only because of their bad mark is and remains highly questionable, especially as there are no direct sanctions involved in non-compliance.

The most important conclusion drawn by Aarts, Burkhauser and De Jong on the basis of their comparative law study of the disability policies in the Netherlands, Germany, Sweden and the United States, is that the difference in numbers of disabled workers in these countries can at least partly be explained by the extent to which financial stimuli are used to influence that number. The recent changes to the Dutch system of social security are clear examples of this idea. In essence these entail a shift in responsibility from government to labour organization. By means of a full range of positive and negative financial stimuli these organizations are pressed to actually take that responsibility. Recent unemployment figures seem to indicate that this method works. Based on this too the authors tend to conclude that a form of structured competition may prove an adequate way to achieve a better balance between equality and efficiency.

It must be pointed out that the crucial question is whether and if, under what conditions, labour organizations will be willing to structure their responsibility for the realization of the reintegration goal. It is as yet to early to know. As a result there is no certainty as regards the adequacy of such policy to reduce the number of beneficiaries. In view of this some restraint seems wise in promoting the Dutch model as an example of an efficient method to curb unemployment among partially disabled people.

Finally, in chapter 8 an attempt is made on the basis of these contributions to provide an answer to the question what factors may help achieve successful reintegration of partially disabled people in the labour process. Different factors can be deduced from these contributions. However, before discussing these in more detail first the contributions are presented. What findings result and what conclusions can be drawn will be discussed in the final chapter.

References

Elshoff, R.P.Th., Reïntegratie in perspectief, Tica symposium, Succesvol reïntegreren: kansen voor de toekomst, Tica, Amsterdam, 1995.

Nijhuis, F.J.N., Reïntegratiebeleid: meer dan herplaatsing!, Tica symposium, Succesvol reïntegreren: kansen voor de toekomst, Tica, Amsterdam, 1995.

Endnote

1. In this book the terms 'reintegration' and 'rehabilitation' are both used. Rehabititation is a general term covering all kinds of measure of a medical, psychological, social or occupational nature which can assist those who are ill or disabled to regain their maximum functional abilities and create conditions required for a normal life. Reintegration refers to the same kind of measures but aims especially at promoting return to the labour process.

Changing the Social Security System into a More Selective System: Stimulus or Obstacle to Reintegration in the Netherlands

Stella den Uijl, Saskia Klosse, Tineke Bahlmann and *Joop Schippers*

1 Introduction

Over the last years the Netherlands have faced a steadily increasing claim on social benefit schemes. Especially the claim on disability schemes is worrying. Attempts to stem the tide undertaken in the Eighties by reducing the levels of benefits were unsuccessful. That is why in the early Nineties a new course was set out. This course was based on strengthening the sense of personal responsibility to cooperate in ensuring the financial feasibility of the social security system. The idea behind this was that the originally existing sense of individual responsibility had been smothered by the all too social and generous system of social security. It is assumed, that if people once more accept their own responsibility they will claim benefits less easily and will get off income support sooner.

As regards the actions taken to achieve this goal two tendencies can be discerned. The first tendency, concerning disability schemes, is the introduction of stricter eligibility requirements. Against this background, the concept of suitable employment has been given a wider interpretation and medical tests have become more strict. Because of these stricter eligibility requirements people will less easily be granted income support and especially young people will have their wage-related benefits replaced by benefits at subsistence level sooner than used to be the case.
Making disability schemes thus less easily accessible is supposed to reduce the influx into these schemes. The general idea behind these changes being that the social security system will then be reserved for those who really need it. This tendency, which amounts to making the social security system more selective, is sometimes described as the evolution from the so-called solidarity-collective model to a market-orientated model. This evolution entails relinquishing the solidarity concept while at the same time increasing the sense of personal responsibility of those concerned to find and keep a job.

The second tendency discernable is the interest for reintegration of partially disabled people in the labour process. In this field, a shift in approach can be observed. After a period of relatively little interest for reintegration we now have a period during which the interest for reintegration is ever increasing.

This has a financial origin. The growing number of people receiving income subsitituting benefits proved too much of a burden for the economy. The social security system as it was had become too expensive. In order to alter this situation, promoting the outflow of partially disabled people from the disability schemes seemed to be the most natural solution. Sprouting from this idea, it seemed necessary to put fresh impetus into reintegration regulations. These regulations must induce employers to employ and retain people with disability benefits.

However, as research shows, very little use has been made of these regulations so far. The fact that until now employers tend to think in terms of production, plays a significant role in this. In actual practice, anyone not productive enough apparently runs the risk of being dismissed and placed under the disability scheme. The question arises how to reconcile this productivity need of employers with the current tendency to enhance reintegration. This seems to be a burning question especially when the tendency of an ever increasing productivity need is combined with the above mentioned evolution of the social security system from a solidarity-collective system to a selective market system. Taking into account that this evolution tends to affect the notion of solidarity, it seems justified to question whether these tendencies will concur at all with the intention to encourage the reintegration of partially disabled people. After all, for reintegration of partially disabled people to succeed, solidarity of employers as regards these disabled becomes a necessity. What solutions does the government present to the problems arising from these two, at first sight, conflicting developments? And will these suffice or should we look for other solutions? These are the topics to be discussed in more depth in this contribution.

2 Evolving from a Solidarity-Collective Model Towards a Selective Market Model

The present Dutch social security system is the result of processes increasing solidarity and collectivity which have taken place in the field of insuring social risks since the last century. This result is also called the solidarity-collective model. Over the past 10 years, however, this model has met with criticism and the selective market model has gained in popularity (Van Oorschot et al., 1996). For a clear understanding of the description and evaluation of these developments it is necessary to first define both the solidarity-collective and the selective market model (cf. Van Oorschot *et al.*, 1996).

2.1 Characteristics of the Solidarity-Collective Model

The solidarity-collective model of social security is characterized by two qualities: increasing solidarity and increasing collectivity. Solidarity may in the widest possible sense be defined as a condition of positive mutual support between individuals or groups. That is to say, as a condition of social relationships being determined by the stronger helping the weaker, or the promotion of shared interests (Van Oorschot *et al.*, 1991). As regards social security this solidarity manifests itself primarily in a redistribution of the costs and profits involved between higher and lower income groups (vertical solidarity) or among groups of individuals with a shared but varying risk (horizontal solidarity).

Collectivity in social insurance involves the social level at which the insurance is organized, the number of different risks covered by that social insurance and the amount of people insured. Making social security a collective affair means that social insurance is organized at a high social level, covering several social risks and large groups of insured or a major part of the national population.
In case solidarity is in essence involved with unequal distribution of costs and profits of the insurance and where increasing solidarity introduces or increases disproportionality, collectivity involves the extent of the population where this solidarity occurs and the social level at which the rules of solidarity are determined. So although solidarity and collectivity are clearly distinguishable, the two usually go together. The key issue is the distribution of risks.

2.2 Characteristics of the Selective Market Model

Characteristic for the selective market model is that social security is organized not by means of solidarity but by means of the principle of equivalence. Social security is thus more selectively organized in the sense that the distribution of costs and profits of insurance are adapted rather more to the individual probability the risk will materialize and the expected extent of the damage. Besides risk selection this model therefore also entails risk differentiation and premium differentiation.
A second characteristic of the selective market model is that the organization of social security is left to the market, that is to say to the interaction of supply and demand between individual citizens, employees and employers on the one hand and

commercial insurers on the other. This entails a vast measure of voluntarism and freedom of choice. The citizen's own responsibility is the key to this model.

Presently, the selective market model predominates. The tendency to increase the citizen's individual responsibility plays an important role here. The shift towards the selective market model, however, is also directly due to dissatisfaction with the solidarity-collective model. That model is no longer considered the best way to offer social protection. The mutually dependent costs and volume issues of social security are more and more related to the collective and solidarity aspects of the model.

The most important objection is considered to be the anonimity of the system. Because of the broad basis for social insurances, at national or branch level, the individual sense of responsibility is supposedly undermined and the calculating attitude of people and organizations is enhanced. Thus, employers and employees are blamed for the fact that in the past the outflow of superfluous workers via the disability scheme was too easily. People had come to regard their premiums more as down payments which entitled them to benefits. Prevention and reintegration were neglected because they were in no one's interest. Because compensation of loss of income was the primary objective, there was no stimulus to promote prevention and reintegration. The solidarity-collective model is so far removed from the insurance principle, it invites, as it were, irresponsible behaviour and further burdening of the collective with the costs ('free rider' behaviour).
The increase in costs in social security is regarded mostly as a result of the ambiguous responsibility structure. The introduction of market economy aspects into social security should redirect the distribution of responsibilities by means of stimuli aimed at personal interests and competition.

A second disadvantage to the solidarity-collective model is that it no longer fits the current concept of the relation government-individual. The model does not fit the tendency towards individualization and freedom of choice. Social security has thus become part of the general reconsideration of key tasks of the government. The opinion that the administration should limit itself to guaranteeing a minimum subsistence level and that obligatory insurance for huge collectivities should be abolished where possible, is gaining ground.

The final argument is that the principle of solidarity has lost much of its legitimacy. On the one hand due to the individualization process and on the other hand because of the growing loss of confidence in the just workings of the scheme. Collective and social regulations would allow too much leeway for incorrect use if not abuse. More in general, therefore, the idea prevails that the link between rights and obligations should be more explicit (Van Oorschot *et al.*, 1996).

3 Better Focus on Reintegration

3.1 Background

The development of the social security system from solidarity-collective model to selective market model also entails that reintegration is seen in a different light. Under the solidarity and collective system reintegration receives barely any attention. Income protection is the prime issue. The stronger must take care of the weaker. Solidarity is apparent in the distribution of profits and costs between higher and lower income groups or among citizens with a shared but varying risk. This leads to high benefits for many people.

Reintegration vanishes against this background. There were, however, also some advantages to contrast this neglect of reintegration which have apparently tipped the scales in their favour for years (Klosse, 1995a). Emphasizing the income compensation function of the system for instance, allowed to sustain a reasonable level of public spending despite an enormous outflow of personnel. Furthermore, this method resulted in high productivity per employee and a large extent of industrial peace. Yet, the price of these advantages proved too high in the end. The steadily growing group of people who were thus removed from the labour market shook the foundations of the social security system.

As a result a shift occured to the opposite. Market mechanism and selectivity became the code words. The citizen's individual responsibility must be stimulated. Furthermore, in order to reestablish the completely upturned balance between the numbers of unemployed and employed, in the early Nineties promotion of labour participation and therefore also of reintegration of partially disabled people is given highest priority (Klosse, 1995b). The administration in doing so explicitly opts for 'work in stead of income subsitution'. With this choice the administration relinquishes the primacy of the compensation function of the security system and replaces it with 'employment'. This from the refreshing point of view that performing paid qualitatively good work is not only the best guarantee against lasting social and financial security, but also offers a stable foundation for quality of life.

Besides personal interests there are also financial motives involved in promoting the reintegration of partially disabled people into the labour process. Meeting the requirements of the EMU with respect to the budget deficit, public finance and inflation called for a substantial reduction of collective expenditures during the last few years. Stimulating reintegration is considered an adequate instrument to favour such a reduction. It is expected that this concept of helping partially disabled employees back to work will decrease the claim made on the social benefits system. Via reduced premiums this will in its turn lead to a reduction of collective expenses or labour costs. This will give a strong impulse to the economy and at the same time improve competitiveness.

Besides for financial reasons the creation of (new) employment, as discussed above, is also considered important in view of the possibilities for self-development and social integration which participation in the labour process offers. The underlying concept is that employment adds meaning to human existence which thus gains new vitality. This means at the same time that reintegration policies cannot take just any form. If one is serious about self-development, governmental policies will have to encompass more than merely creating more jobs. Those jobs also have to offer possibilities for self-development and will therefore have to meet certain quality requirements. This means that participation policies will have to be organized in a way that creates more high quality jobs. This also seems to concur with the above mentioned point of view that performance of high quality work is the foundation for good quality of life and also provides a guarantee for lasting social security.

3.2 Ways to Promote Reintegration

It follows from the above that advancing reintegration will have to balance between quantity in view of competitiveness and the economic basis, and quality in view of the quality of life and lasting social security. Whether and if, to what degree this balance will be realized, depends on the means available. Is it possible to reach this goal of self-development and the change to the selective market model at the same time? In order to find an answer to this last question it is necessary to take a closer look at the regulations aimed at advancing reintegration. Two possible means are indicated: increasing employment possibilities and extending reintegration regulations.

3.2.1 Increasing Employment Possibilities
Alongside a number of measures that aim to improve the availability of unemployed for the labour market another package of measures is proposed which aim at (re)activating the demand for low productive labour on which most partially disabled

people depend. This is necessary because many of the jobs they depend on have disappeared over the years. The steadily increasing claim on the benefit system and the related increase in labour costs are the cause of this.

In order to reactivate the demand for this kind of labour a reduction of labour costs seems the logical option. It is not hard to trace the reason behind this solution. We cannot ignore the fact that large numbers of workers and their jobs have been priced out of the market over the years. All kinds of services have disappeared because they became too expensive due to ever higher labour costs. So, if you make labour cheaper the demand for this kind of work will increase and the jobs that have disappeared might be recreated.

This can be achieved in various ways. One of those is to grant certain sectors dispensation from the *Wet op het minimumloon* (Minimum Wage Act) for a specific period. Without infringing on the statutory minimum wages the possibility is thus created to adequately and temporarily relief employers of their obligation to pay minimum wages. This measure is expected to increase the demand for low productive labour. A comparable regulation, the *Wet loonkostenreductie op minimumloonniveau* (Labour cost reduction at minimum level), has recently been abolished so some qualification of this expectation seems called for. In practice hardly any employers applied for this regulation because most of them are bound by wages stipulated in collective labour agreements which (far) exceed the statutory minimum wages. This fact has been taken into account in this new regulation in so far that the above dispensation must be supplemented with run-in wage scales for employees with insufficient work experience. Thus the aim is to offer the perspective of people gaining further qualifications for the labour market by working.

The so-called 'Melkert-jobs' are another way to increase employment for people currently on income support. They are part of the employment policy of the government. These jobs are mostly government jobs paid out of collective means which harbours several dangers such as distorting competition and replacing non-subsidized employees by subsidized ones.

However, these dangers which may undermine a lasting reintegration in the labour process, are contrasted by some advantages. Thus, for instance, the unemployed which are in this way helped to a job, get the opportunity to prove themselves valuable workers in the labour market and, furthermore, to earn an independent income at minimum level or slightly above. In turn this may help prevent the development of a social dichotomy. In view of the importance of these advantages it seems advisable to make good use of this regulation, for instance by finding adequate ways in which to avoid the aforementioned disadvantages.

Bearing in mind that obtaining paid work in the labour market is still no feasible option for everybody despite the aforementioned measures, an alternative route has been set out. However, this option is open only to those who have been on income support for at least twelve months and whose chances of returning to the labour market are rather small. They are allowed to perform certain socially useful tasks while retaining their right to benefits.

The aim of this regulation is to allow these people to get some work experience (in advance) so as to better qualify for a return to paid labour and thus to enable them to gain employee status in the end. More concretely this is organized by relieving unemployed that belong to the group targeted by this regulation from certain obligations linked to the right to social benefits, such as obligatory application for jobs. However, this is replaced by another obligation namely that of being socially useful in an as such acknowledged form, or forfeit the right to income support. This obligation is justified by invoking the good causes served by this form of employment. It is for instance expected that this will help prevent people getting socially isolated and, furthermore, that in this way a contribution is made to preventing social exclusion and the development of a social dichotomy. Entirely in line with the activation idea there is also the claim on the 'no free lunch'-principle which neatly fits in with market concepts. In return for the benefits they receive these people have to 'earn' their allowances by being useful to society or lose their benefits.

In view of the fact that until now the unemployed were not allowed to make themselves thus useful, this looks like a u-turn. However, even though benefit claimants are now offered wider possibilities to do something for society this is still treated as the exception rather than the rule. Besides the fact that this possibility is limited to certain groups of unemployed, this is also apparent from the fact that only work which is officially recognized as socially useful may be performed. This shows that the government intends to keep the possibility to work while retaining income support as small as possible and, in relation, to primarily aim at reintroduction in the paid labour market.

3.2.2 Specific Reintegration Regulations

Besides (re)activating the demand for low productive labour, specific reintegration regulations have been introduced to stimulate the advancement of partially disabled people in the labour market. Some of these regulations aim at reducing the volume of disability benefits (volume acts) and some aim at improving the labour market position of the partially disabled (supplementary policy) (Baar, 1996). Within this supplementary policy a number of specific reintegration regulations have been developed. Thus, for instance, there is the possibility for employers to be relieved of the obligation to pay seventy per cent of the wages in case the partially disabled employee falls ill (Article 29b ZW, Health Act). Costs incurred in providing an adapted work space can also be recovered (Articles 2 WAGW and 57/57a AAW). An attempt has been made to remove obstacles for the employer to employing a partially disabled employee in providing wage dispensation (Article 8 WAGW), labour cost subsidies (Article 62 WAO) and the possibility of trial employment (Article 63 WAO). Regulations specifically intended to remove obstacles for the partially disabled employee himself are wage supplements (Article 60 WAO) and a guarantee regulation for older employees (Article 61 WAO).

4 Comments on the Policy to Encourage Reintegration

Unfortunately, recent research by the monitoring authority on social security Ctsv (1995) has proven that the various reintegration regulations and especially the positive stimuli for employers such as labour cost subsidies and the possibility to be relieved of the obligation to pay seventy per cent of wages in case a partially disabled employee falls ill (Article 29b ZW) have had very little effect. The *Nationale Comité Chronisch Zieken* (National Committee for the Chronically Ill) (1995) also notes that the reintegration regulations are insufficiently used. Employers for instance hardly ever claim compensation for education and work adaptation costs, whereas the majority of partially disabled people needs these provisions in order to perform well.

It is assumed that unfamiliarity of the partially disabled person with the various regulations may lead to limited application. Added to that is the fact that although the implementing organizations in principle inform those concerned about the regulations, employers too are often unaware of the possibilities. As the employer himself will have to apply for these subsidies, this unawareness of the regulations constitutes a significant obstruction to proper reintegration. Another reason for the limited use made of the regulations is that many employers feel no need for them, as well as being worried about the 'red tape' involved and some problems are caused by the ever changing and divided legislation.

However, the most structural reason for limited use is the aspect of risk selection (Ctsv, 1995). Employers are primarily interested in a good candidate for the job. Candidates with a history of (partial) disability are therefore easily excluded also because of negative stimuli (risk selection). Positive incentives affect hardly any change in employer attitudes (Ctsv, 1996). Such positive stimuli may manage to finally convince employers who are considering employing partially disabled workers anyhow (labour cost subsidy, Article 29b ZW). Yet, the negative stimulus of risk selection in general proves stronger than the positive stimulus of reintegration regulations.

From this it seems to follow that positive stimuli, such as labour cost subsidies, trial employment, wage supplements and provisions like Article 29b ZW, are no convincing incentives for employers. In spite of these measures they apparently continue to prefer healthy employees to employees for which one expects a high drop-out risk.

Partially disabled people are faced with a number of other problems as well. So, for instance, it appears that despite employment protection employers may easily dismiss a partially disabled worker. Due to the negative financial incentives employers tend to do this increasingly often (increase in outflow selection). In case employment is retained there may be a problem regarding repositioning. Due to the huge number that need to be repositioned, finding new adequate functions is no easy task. This is complicated by the fact that the group of people the employer has to reposition has grown since employees who are less than fifteen per cent disabled must also be found suitable jobs. The low number of work adaptations too constitutes a pressure point because it results in inferior quality of work and in turn in higher rates of absence from work. Prejudices and lack of knowledge on the part of both employer and colleagues will also pose a problem to the partially disabled person. The prejudices may cause stress because he or she does not want to confirm these and will therefore exert him or herself too much. Even outside the labour process the partially disabled worker will run into trouble. Extended influx selection has increased and obstructs the access to labour. The vast group of formerly disabled people in the labour market (due to the stricter medical checks) also constitutes a hurdle on the way to work.

The introduction of more market economy aspects and selectivity into the social security system enhances these effects. Introducing these aspects will probably lead to an increase in risk selection by employers 'at the gate'. This will make it even more difficult for the partially disabled worker to find and keep a job. Even 'inside the gate' sick leave and disability will be dealt with more strictly. This may lead to an earlier outflow of high risk employees.

More premium differentiation may lead to higher costs for companies with a high percentage of sick leave. Increased risk and premium differentiation will result in more selective protection and to larger differences between groups of employees. Employees at work in companies with high risks will have to pay more premium for their insurances. To what extent these possibilities will materialize, depends on, among other things, the power and influence of the various employee organizations.

Increased risk differentiation may also change the social economic structure. 'Sick' businesses lose out to more healthy companies. All in all one may say that extensive application of the selective market model, as the government plans to as regards short and long term disability, will for one reason or another lead to shifts in the protection of groups of workers and in the financial burdens for companies. There is as yet little information on the direction and extent of such shifts but it looks as if particularly partially disabled people and small businesses will lose out in the end. There is insufficient information on whether the intended effect of volume management and reduction will occur in any significant proportion. The chance of unintended, unwanted consequences occurring is therefore quite significant. In this context we may point out the expected strict selection of employees 'at' and 'inside' the gate which will result in more inequality in the labour market. This will entail a deterioration of the market position of weaker groups, and will eventually lead to further social inequality and injustice.

To our opinion sound policies primarily need sound and extensive investigation of the actual effects that can be expected when implementing the government's plans. If not, the execution of these plans is a shot in the dark with unknown consequences. One may certainly expect that as a result of the deterioration of the labour market positions of weaker groups, government policy as regards reintegration will have to be expanded both in terms of legislation and in terms of the financial means needed for execution. This effect has until now failed to receive enough attention.

5 Complementary Measures

The government realizes that the unwanted side effect of increased risk selection may occur as a result of the new policy to make the social security system more selective and more market-oriented. This will further hamper access to the labour market for partially disabled people. The government will therefore expand the supplementary regulations it had already initiated in order to curb this increased risk selection.
For this purpose the statutory reintegration regulations such as wage supplements, labour cost subsidies, trial employment and the guarantee regulation for older employees will be extended. The government intends to add to these regulations a premium reduction for chronically ill people, an evaluation of the extent to which risk selection actually occurs, introduction of an information centre for recruiting and selection, counselling and expertise promotion, and combining the reintegration regulations in a *Wet op de reintegratie* (Reintegration Act).

Improvement of the regulations might get more employers interested in reintegration and this would reduce the hurdle of the currently insufficient use of reintegration regulations.

However, one must realize that the question remains whether improving and renewing the regulations will prove a solution to the problem of insufficient use. After all, one of the reasons for insufficient use is the fact that there seems to be little call for these regulations. The most important reason for the waste is, as was discussed above, the fact that the negative incentives are stronger than the positive ones to stimulate real reintegration.

Given this context, the question arises what factors do have a positive influence on the selection behaviour of employers? Research shows that a number of factors play a role in this respect (Mul *et al.*, 1995). These are the employer's opinion on reintegration, his expectation as regards the level of performance of partially disabled people, information, the employer's policy, and the willingness of the organization to adapt the work.

From this it follows that in the first place the employer's idea of reintegration colours his selection behaviour. This comprises a positive or negative attitude towards partially disabled people and sometimes the prejudices regarding them. Whether the employer has personally had any positive, negative or no experiences with partially disabled people determines to some extent his attitude towards this group.

Any negative expectations on the part of the employer as regards the level of performance of partially disabled people also decides the former's selection: fear of insufficient knowledge and skills. This leads to fear of insufficient performance and insufficient productivity. This is aggravated by the fear for negative reactions from the customers and expected high sick leave and disability risks.

The information and policy of the employer are in turn determined by other factors: familiarity with the regulations, pursuing a systematic policy as regards hiring partially disabled employees, active social-medical supervision and cooperation with the implementing organization.

As far as the organization of work is concerned this depends on whether the employer is willing to make the work more accessible by creating individual suitable tasks, that is adapting working hours, adapting job criteria and implementing technical adaptations.

This set of four factors, the employer's frame of mind, his expectation as regards productivity of the partially disabled worker, his information and policy and the willingness to adapt the work, are mutually related. The overall attitude of the employer as regards partially disabled people determines his specific expectations of them. These two factors then determine his policy as regards hiring or not hiring people with limitations. If the policy is positive, then structuring and possible adaptation of the work become feasible. It is very important that these factors are taken into account when developing and implementing policies that aim to encourage the reintegration of partially disabled people.

6 Conclusions

History teaches us two things regarding reintegration policies concerning partially disabled people. Primarily that in times of labour shortage, when the demand for labour exceeds the supply, reintegration is considered very important. Thus, following the Second World War reintegration was high on everybody's agenda. Anyone who could work was to be recruited. Secondly, the costs involved play an important role in the decision whether or not to promote reintegration. The Dutch state could not afford the situation where war veterans merely claimed benefits and remained unproductive. By the time economic growth came to a halt and the shortage of labour turned into a surplus, the urge to reintegrate was completely lost. The economic developments of the Seventies at the time of economic depression show the same development.

From this it follows that social responsibility is very susceptible to economic trends. But what consequences has this policy had for the Dutch economy? Was it realistic to promote reintegration at times of prosperity and ignoring it at times of depression? Such policies also have a down side. The result is that in the Netherlands there is an ever growing group of people depending on income support rather than on wages. The question arises whether changing the social security system into a selective market model is a solution to this problem. The development into this direction has resulted in bringing reintegration back on the political agenda, but it also entails a number of disadvantages such as risk selection and negative consequences for small businesses due to premium differentiation. This results in reduced solidarity. Yet, for reintegration to be a success this solidarity at company level should increase, not decrease. The Dutch government must try and prevent the negative consequences of the selective market model prevailing in a number of years time, which would in the end lead to the reintroduction of solidarity-collective model. It will be better to strike a balance between solidarity and market economy than to exchange one model for the other, which is what has happened until now (Oudshoorn and Vijlbrief, 1995).

This will not be an easy thing to achieve in view of the economic climate which continuously demands higher productivity. The idea of reintegrating partially disabled people does not fit in with the competitive structure of modern society. This must be kept in mind when implementing regulations to promote reintegration as is clear in relation to at least one of the solutions, the introduction of all sorts of positive stimuli to bring about reintegration. Under the current circumstances the question whether or not to hire someone is decided by his or her expected productivity: jobs must be cost effective. It seems unlikely that this notion will change due to positive financial stimuli because these do not meet the productivity requirements. For this reason, it is doubtful to what extent these incentives will induce employers to hire partially disabled employees. The fact is that employers think that especially the partially disabled will fail to meet productivity requirements. Positive stimuli, such as all sorts of subsidies, are not the best means by which to change this situation. Without a change in the economic climate employers will continue to try and deny their responsibility for reintegrating partially disabled people as much as possible by stating that there is no suitable work available for them in the company.

The second problem that has been underestimated is the fact that a large number of disabled workers for whose benefit these measures are intended, have been excluded from the labour market for many years now. Besides the fact that they do not have the right qualifications they were written off in the past as obsolete machinery. The question is whether and if, how this situation can be drastically changed. For some of them of course the gap between demand and supply can be bridged with specific training. Some will be able to find a suitable job through intensive mediation, re-entry programmes and active labour market policies. Subsidies and other positive stimuli may help to achieve that goal, but only as supplementary measures. The first thing to do is to make partially disabled employees ready for the labour market. As long as that has not been achieved, positive stimuli easily will miss their target.

And yet, it must be kept in mind that all this only applies to a specific group among the disabled, namely the young ones and those that have not yet been disabled for any length of time. Despite the pressure, though, a large group of them will still be very difficult to place. The majority will have to aim for unskilled or lowskilled jobs, but their chances of being actually employed for this kind of work are very low as long as their productivity is less than their costs. It is highly unlikely that this situation will change by promoting reintegration. As these people have been excluded from the labour market for many years one may wonder whether there is any regulation that can promote their reintegration. Is it not a fact of life that if one wishes to reintegrate someone this process should be started as early as possible? The longer the reintegration process lasts, the less chance of success.

The problem remains of how to achieve solidarity at company level. How to convince employers that partially disabled people can be quite productive? What can the government do about employers' prejudices as regards the productivity of the partially disabled? It will be clear that this cannot be done by abolishing solidarity. By emphasizing the personal responsibility of employers and employees the government has knocked the principle of solidarity right on the head, whereas it is precisely this solidarity that allows the partially disabled to participate in the labour market. We do not refer to pecuniary solidarity (income replacement benefits) but to genuine solidarity (actual reintegration). That requires a change of opinion on the part of the employers. But what means should the government choose with which to achieve this change of heart?

The answer to this question may be found by taking several possibilities into consideration. One of them is to put less emphasis on reducing the costs of the social security scheme, and more emphasis on influencing the employers' perception of reality as regards the productivity that partially disabled people may have. This shift in emphasis would be very important to partially disabled workers. An important option in this is to stress the partially disabled's motivation for work. Highly motivated people are very important to an employer for the success of his company. Employers must be convinced of the fact that reintegrated partially disabled employees are not per definition demotivated and frequently ill. The employer's experience with partially disabled people is decisive in this matter and this is where the government comes in. Primarily it should set a good example. At the moment the government employs the smallest percentage of partially disabled people as compared to the various industrial branches. To present a convincing labour market policy, this should be the first step. Work experience positions, apprenticeships *et cetera* for the partially disabled with various employers would also help to convince the latter. Thus, they can gain experience in working with partially disabled people and form a more positive idea of this group. This could put an end to the process of keeping partially disabled people out of doors because of suspected reduced productivity.

In the Netherlands there is only very little research available on what factors contribute to successful reintegration of partially disabled people in the labour process at company level, including the effects of regulations in as far as this concerns the situation within the company. These days it seems that the means to increase labour participation of partially disabled people is found in increasing the responsibility of individual employers and employees. Whether this is the best way in which to enhance reintegration will only be known once there is sufficient insight into the factors that contribute to successful reintegration. Research into the attitudes of employers and employees as regards partially disabled workers is therefore very important.

References

Baar, E., De arbeidsmarktpositie van werknemers met een arbeidshandicap: knelpunten en mogelijke oplossingen, Afstudeerscriptie RGL, Universiteit Utrecht, 1996.

College van Toezicht Sociale Verzekeringen, Risicoselectie op de Nederlandse arbeidsmarkt: selectieve aanstelling en afvloeiing van personeel op grond van (vermeende) risico's binnen de Ziektewet en de WAO, Zoetermeer, 1995.

College van Toezicht Sociale verzekeringen, Toepassing van reïntegratie-instrumenten voor gedeeltelijk arbeidsgeschikten, Zoetermeer, 1996.

Klosse, S., Reintegration of beneficiaries, Guest lecture, Oslo, 1995(a).

Klosse, S., Bevordering van arbeidsparticipatie ofwel: werk boven 'wig' of 'wig' boven werk?, Samsom H.D. Tjeenk Willink, Alphen aan den Rijn, 1995(b).

Mul, C.A.M., C.R. Winter, I.D. de Nijboer, H.F. de Haan, Methoden voor de (re-)integratie van gedeeltelijk arbeidsgeschikten, Vuga, Den Haag, 1995.

Nationale Commissie Chronisch Zieken, Advies privatisering Ziektewet, opting-out/premiedifferentiatie WAO en de consequenties voor mensen met een arbeidshandicap, Zoetermeer, 1995.

Oorschot, W. van, Solidariteit in verzekering en sociale zekerheid: analyse van een begrip, Sociaal Maandblad Arbeid, 1991, jrg 46 vol. 7/8, p. 358-374.

Oorschot, W. van, C. Boos, L. Geleijnse, Solidair of selectief, Kluwer/SOVAC, Deventer/Utrecht, 1996.

Oudshoorn, C., J.A. Vijlbrief, Nieuwe wegen naar sociale en economische vooruitgang, Economisch-Statische Berichten, 1995, jrg 80, nr. 4024.

The Rehabilitation of Partially Disabled Workers in Sweden

Lotta Westerhäll

1 Background

Long-term absence from work due to sickness has increased during the last decades. This is true particularly for such absence which is compensated by supplementary disability pension or sick-benefit. Between 1963 and 1993, the percentage of the population receiving such compensation increased from 3.0 to 7.3%. The number of employed citizens per disability pensioner decreased from 25 to 10. It should be noted that this development occurred during a period when the general age of retirement was changed from 67 to 65 years of age.

During the 1980s, the absence from work due to sickness increased considerably. The number of persons receiving supplementary disability pension or sick-benefit for cases of illness lasting longer than twelve months increased from 311,000 to 436,000 between 1980 and 1990.

In the early 1990s, several measures were taken with the purpose of getting better grip on insurance costs and creating a more efficient insurance. The levels for compensation in the sick-benefit insurance were lowered. A qualifying period of one day was introduced, as well as sickness payment. The employers were prescribed by law a responsibility for rehabilitation. The individual's responsibility for his own rehabilitation was increased. Social insurance organizations were given the role of coordinators. The concept of work injury was changed and the right to work injury allowance was practically abolished. Within the field of disability pensions, the possibility of receiving such pension for isolated labour market reasons was abolished and a larger number of sickness pension categories were introduced. At the same time, the Swedish economy landed in a major depression.

Absence from work due to sickness decreased in the first half of the 1990s. The number of cases of short and average length was reduced. The trend of rapidly increasing long-term cases was broken. The sum of the number of supplementary disability pensions/sick-benefits and of current compensation cases lasting longer than twelve months was 458,000 in December 1994. Since the number of part-time pensioners and part-time sick-listed persons increased during the same period, a

27

recalculation into whole-year pensions/sick-listings would have shown the break in trend in 1994 even clearer. The high number of disability pensions in 1992 and 1993 was thus mainly a transference from long time sick-benefit cases into disability pensions. The number of persons receiving sick-benefit or rehabilitation compensation for more than one year seems to have halted at a level of 45,000 since the middle of 1994. At present, the number of newly granted disability pensions/sick-benefits is decreasing, and the Swedish National Social Insurance Board estimates a number of about 40,000 during 1995. Long-time absence from work due to sickness thus seems to have stagnated.

During the 1980s, several large commissions were undertaken in order to adapt rules and work to the changed circumstances.

In the Government's proposition 1990/91: 140 'Working environment and rehabilitation', the Chief of the Ministry of Health and Social Welfare basically follows the proposition of the Working Environment Commission. The employees are granted the right to a comprehensive and developing job, and a possibility to influence changes and development. The concept of working environment is expanded to cover the technique and the organisation and contents of the work. One shall strive to attain possibilities of variation, social contact, cooperation and coherence between different assignments. Strictly governed and confined work shall be avoided as far as possible. The employer has the responsibility to plan systematically, to lead and control the striving for a better environment, and to see to it that there is always a suitably organised action for adjustment and rehabilitation. The demand to adjust the working conditions to the individual employee is made clearer.

In the Government's Proposition 1990/91: 140 'Working environment and rehabilitation', the Chief of the Ministry states: 'The social insurance system must be given the same evident active shaping as the labour market politics. The focus of the rehabilitation process shall be pushed towards working life.' It is suggested in the proposition that the employer shall have the responsibility to elucidate the employee's rehabilitation requirements and to take the measures needed for occupationally oriented rehabilitation. This proposition thus forms the ground for the rules about rehabilitation in chapter 22 in the National Insurance Act, which came into effect in January 1992.

2 Rehabilitation in Sweden in General

2.1 What is Rehabilitation?

Those who have been on sick-leave occasionally require assistance to resume work. Rehabilitation is a general term covering all forms of measures of a medical, psychological, social and occupational nature, which can assist those who have been ill or injured to regain the maximum functional ability and create the conditions required for a normal life. Different authorities, or principals, are responsible for the various areas.

The public health authorities are responsible for medical rehabilitation, whereas the municipal/social services are in charge of the social aspects. Responsibility for occupational rehabilitation is shared by the labour market authorities, the social insurance organization and the employer. The responsibility for coordination rests with the social insurance organization.

Occupationally oriented rehabilitation refers to the measures required to assist an absentee to regain his capacity to work, thereby creating the conditions required to support himself through gainful employment.

The employer is primarily responsible for identifying and determining the need for rehabilitation, for ensuring that measures are introduced, and for financing these measures. Financial responsibility is, however, limited to measures that can be taken within, or in conjunction with, the framework of the company's operations.

The employee should be offered continued employment by the employer, and other alternatives should be explored only when this possibility is exhausted.

Experience confirms that it is important to commence rehabilitation as soon as possible in order to ensure successful results. Moreover, when a rehabilitation requirement is identified at an early stage, it can be remedied more easily than when it has existed for a long time.

In general, the workplace offers the best conditions for successful rehabilitation. The absentee is familiar with this environment and can receive assistance from colleagues and trade union representatives.

To ensure that the necessary rehabilitation commences as soon as possible, the employer is obliged to consult the employee and, if required, conduct a rehabilitation inquiry when

– the employee has been ill for more than four weeks in succession;

- the employee has been ill on six occasions or more during the last 12-month period;
- the employee requests such an inquiry.

The purpose of the rehabilitation inquiry is to identify the rehabilitation requirements. The employer is also obliged to assume responsibility for rehabilitation measures that can be conducted within, or in connection with, the company's operations. This may involve

- modifications of the workplace;
- changes in tasks/redeployment;
- changes in working hours;
- job testing/job training;
- education.

What is regarded as reasonable to demand from a particular employer varies from case to case. Both the employer's and the employee's circumstances must be taken into account.

As long as the employee is on sick-leave or is receiving sick pay, he is entitled to retain his position.

2.2 The Responsibilities of the Employee and the Social Insurance Organization

An employee who has been ill for more than four weeks must submit a medical certificate to the social insurance organization. The medical certificate should state the employee's rehabilitation requirements and how long he is expected to remain on sick-leave.

The employee is also responsible for

- submitting the information required to identify the need for rehabilitation;
- participating in the inquiry and the planning of suitable rehabilitation measures;
- participating in rehabilitation to the best of his ability;
- notifying the social insurance organization of changes in circumstances that determine the entitlement to or the amount of rehabilitation compensation.

The social insurance organization shall coordinate and supervise the measures required for the rehabilitation of the absentee. The social insurance organization shall also take the initiative to rehabilitation measures when this is required. This means, for example, that the social insurance organization shall contact the employer if a rehabilitation inquiry has not been received although the insurance organization believes that an inquiry ought to be prepared.

In cooperation with the absentee, the insurance organization shall draw up a rehabilitation plan. The plan shall comprise the measures required to assure that he can return to work. The employer's rehabilitation inquiry and the medical assessment, combined with the individual understanding the situation, are the most important factors underlying the rehabilitation plan. The social insurance organization is responsible for planning rehabilitation, even for those who require rehabilitation but who are not employed.

The social insurance organization also functions as a representative on behalf of the individual. This means that, when required, the social insurance organization should assist the individual in contacts with authorities and others so that he receives help with the necessary rehabilitation.

Finally, the social insurance organization also evaluates the employee's entitlement to sick-benefit and rehabilitation compensation, and is responsible for payments as well. The social insurance organization may finance occupationally oriented rehabilitation measures in the absence of alternative means of finance.

2.3 Compensation During Rehabilitation

Those participating in occupationally oriented rehabilitation are entitled to reha-bilitation compensation. Rehabilitation compensation consists of two components: Rehabilitation payments designed to cover the loss of income due to the person's participation in rehabilitation, and a special contribution designed to cover certain expenses that arise in conjunction with rehabilitation. Occupationally oriented rehabilitation refers to measures necessary to enable a person to find employment, e.g. job testing, job training and education.

To be entitled to rehabilitation compensation, an application must be submitted to the social insurance organization. Rehabilitation measures must also be included in any plan drawn up by the insurance organization.

Compensation for rehabilitation is slightly higher than sick-benefit in order to stimulate the absentee to seek rehabilitation. It is 100% of the base amount for sick-benefit, whereas sick-benefit for longer periods of illness amounts only to 90%. Rehabilitation compensation can be paid in the form of 100, 75, 50 and 25% compensation. For example, a person who is able to work a maximum of 50% of his ordinary working hours, receives a 50% compensation, while a person who works a maximum of 25% of his normal working hours receives 75% rehabilitation compensation and so on.

A special contribution is paid to cover certain expenses that may arise from participating in occupationally oriented rehabilitation schemes. For instance, a contribution can be paid in the form of travel cost reimbursements and compensation

31

for other expenses if a person is compelled to reside outside his home area. Compensation can also be paid for training materials and course fees.

2.4 Job Training and Work Aids

To facilitate the absentee's return to work, rehabilitation compensation during job training is possible. Job training is a measure on which the absentee, the employer, the physician in charge and the social insurance organization reach an agreement. Training must take place with the person's employer or with some other employer. It is important that the social insurance organization is involved in the discussions at an early stage in order to assist the planning of the training period. The insurance organization can also provide information concerning the requirements for rehabilitation compensation.

Job training may be suitable for those who need to test whether or not they can cope with their work tasks following an accident or illness. Training can begin on a small scale, meaning a few hours a day, and increase steadily. It can also proceed over a number of days, e.g. if a person wishes to see if he can cope with a new job to which he could be transferred. This means that the person enhances his working capacity gradually without being subject to the pressure of piece-rates or normal working hours.

Job training can also be suitable for those who need to test whether they can cope with new tasks by means of work aids or similar utilities.

To be entitled to rehabilitation compensation during the training period, the measures must be included in a rehabilitation plan.

The social insurance organization can contribute to the costs of work aids for those suffering from a functional disability or who have been adversely affected by a long-term illness. The contribution can be made either to the employee or the employer. Work aids include technical devices and special equipment at the workplace. These may be personal or connected with the workplace.

Those who are gainfully employed or have a functional disability which makes it difficult to cope with their work, can receive a contribution from the social insurance organization towards covering the cost of work aids and a modification of the workplace.

Contributions to cover the costs of work aids can also be provided as part of the rehabilitation programme. Contributions are available for work aids that can help to break a protracted period of illness, thereby enabling the absentee to return to work.

In addition, those who are not on sick-benefit can receive a contribution for the necessary work aids in order to obtain or maintain employment.

2.5 Other Measures

The rehabilitation objective of health and medical care is to help the person to regain functional ability to the maximum degree possible. Rehabilitation can also aim at improving a disability or developing compensatory functions.

While a person receives care for his illness/accident, he may at the same time need other forms of assistance from the public health authorities. He can receive treatment from a physiotherapist, occupational therapist, psychologist et cetera. In certain counties the treatment of spinal and neck injuries is facilitated, for example, in addition to activation courses arranged by the public health authorities.

A social welfare officer can help with such social matters such as housing, travel services, home help, equipment to alleviate everyday problems, and financial counselling. The social welfare officer can assist in contacts with other authorities or organizations if so required.

The primary task of the employment office is to assist the unemployed to find new employment. The employment office also assists with occupational counselling.

Many people looking for a job require more assistance to return to the labour market than that provided by the employment office. For a person requiring such assistance, the Labour Market Institutes (AMI) provide occupationally oriented rehabilitation and more advanced counselling. An important part of the AMI operations consists of job testing, which is conducted both at the institute and at workplaces outside the institute. Each county has a Labour Market Institute.

Those participating in rehabilitation are in certain cases entitled to educational grants during the period. An application for these grants can be made through the employment office.

Financial and personal assistance is available from the social welfare office in the municipality. The social welfare office can act as an intermediary for contacts and services from other authorities, and assumes responsibility for the needs, support and assistance which are not provided by any other authority.

For example, one may receive child care facilities, home help and travel services. Occasionally, the social welfare office can also assist in finding a suitable home.

Those who have problems with drugs or alcohol, other social problems, can receive help to overcome these difficulties.

One can also turn to the social welfare office for information concerning the various forms of assistance that are available in one's own municipality.

3 Rehabilitation by the National Insurance Organization During 1986-1991

In the publication 'The Swedish National Social Insurance Board Accounts 1994:5', rehabilitation work by the social insurance organization is described. The material which has been used for the study covers the period 1986-1991, and has been collected from the local social insurance organizations. About 2,800 persons with 4,300 long-term sick-listings (at least 60 days) are included in the investigation. The efforts made by the social insurance organizations in these long-term sick-listings are illustrated. The study includes efforts for rehabilitation which have been initiated by the social insurance organization, rehabilitation work of which the insurance organization has been a part, and measures of which the insurance organization has been informed but in which it did not take part actively.

Between the years 1986 and 1991, efforts to rehabilitate were initiated in 14% of the long-term sick-listings. National statistics show that 900,000 persons together are responsible for 1.4 million sick-listings lasting at least 60 days during the years 1986-1991. According to the social insurance organization's records, rehabilitation work occurred in about 196,000 of these cases. In the light of the facts that the sick-listings which have been studied have lasted for at least 60 days, that 42% of the cases have lasted for more than six months, and that over 40% of the cases concern some kind of illness affecting the movement organs, only 14% starting rehabilitation must be considered a small group. The low percentage of persons on sick-leave going into rehabilitation gives rise to two questions:
– What does the group starting rehabilitation look like?
– What factors increase the plausibility of starting rehabilitation?

The group of people starting rehabilitation differed from the rest of the group of persons on long-term sick-leave in several ways. The persons in the group entering rehabilitation were most often sick-listed due to problems with the movement organs. The age group most frequently affected were persons between 40 and 49 years of age. It was more common for persons in the rehabilitation group to have reported a work injury. It was also more common with sick-listing periods of over one year in the rehabilitation group.

What factors or qualities among long-term sick-listed persons affect their possibilities for rehabilitation? An application or trial for sickness allowance or disability pension decreases the prospect of rehabilitation with 50%.

Compared to persons between 18 and 29 years of age, the age group between 50 and 57 years had a 50% chance of rehabilitation whereas for 58 years old and over, rehabilitation chances were almost non-existent.

The longer the period of sick-listing, the greater the chance of rehabilitation. After 180-365 days on the sick-list, the chances of successful rehabilitation increased six times compared to a sick-listing lasting only 60-89 days.

The diagnosis of the illness behind the sick-leave did not affect the chances for rehabilitation.

A report of work injury doubled the chances of rehabilitation. The fact that the rehabilitation process proceeds faster in these cases, both as regards the contacts the social insurance organization makes with the purpose of investigating the rehabilitation requirements, and as regards the time it takes before rehabilitation measures are started, contradicts the statement that work injury insurance would have an impeding effect on the rehabilitation process.

There are differences in the rehabilitation work depending on the parts involved. The enterprise health care can be taken as an example. The percentage of persons starting rehabilitation is much higher among those where the enterprise health care has been involved in the rehabilitation process than in other groups.

The number of cases where the enterprise health care tried to initiate rehabilitation was, however, very small. The large number of gainfully employed connected to the enterprise health care during the time of the study gives rise to the question whether enterprise health care should have taken the initiative to rehabilitation in more cases. In this context, it should also be mentioned that the number of rehabilitation measures taken by the enterprise health care had decreased considerably during the period 1986-1991 compared to the years 1979-1985 – from 3,000 measures to 400.

Various reasons may interfere with the appointed civil servant continuing to work with the sick-listed person. In only one third of the cases with which the social insurance organization has been in contact, the civil servant has had the chance to work out a rehabilitation plan. In the remaining number of cases, medical or other impediments have been present according to the civil servant. During a two-year period, only a few persons among the cases with medical impediments started rehabilitation. Twice as many persons in the same group received full disability pension or full sick-benefit.

There are several reasons to believe that the group of people whom the civil servants at the social insurance organization meet, differs from the one with whom the enterprise health care works in contexts of rehabilitation. Similar facts are to be found concerning impulses to rehabilitation, that is, the signals that shall initiate an inquiry into rehabilitation requirements.

The sick-listed persons had to wait for a long time before they or another rehabilitation actor were contacted by the social insurance organization to examine whether they were in need of rehabilitation. After three months, only 15% had been contacted to discuss rehabilitation, and less than 3% had started some kind of rehabilitation measure. After one year, a little over 60% of those who were still on the sick-list had been contacted by the social insurance organization, and about 20% had started rehabilitation.

4 The Work of Rehabilitation in the Social Insurance Organization During 1991-1994

4.1 The Purpose and Structure of the Study

Another publication by the Swedish National Social Insurance Board: 'the Swedish National Social Board Accounts 1995:20', or the so-called National Long-term Sick-listing, contains material from a study about long-term sick-listing and rehabilitation. Every local social insurance organization in Sweden except the ones in the county of Stockholm has taken part in the investigation. Sick-listings starting between 1st July 1991 and 30th June 1994 and lasting at least 60 days were selected and studied. The selection was based on data from the Swedish National Social Insurance Board's central computer in Sundsvall. For the results to be meaningful on local level, the study comprised 210 cases per local office. The Stockholm social insurance organization, however, only took part to a limited extent and collected just 10% of the selection, i.e. 21 cases per office. That is an insufficient number for analysis. For the offices in the rest of the country, the 210 cases per office enable a rather thorough investigation. A total of 64,000 cases were included in the national study. The report's purpose is to give a brief and clear picture of the work at the social insurance organizations between 1991 and 1994. The presentation of the study has been split into two periods, namely 1991-1992 and 1993-1994, in order to enable a comparison of the changes that have occurred between the two periods. Wherever possible, comparisons with the period 1986-1991 have also been made.

4.2 Some Results from the Investigation

The long-term sick-listed persons differed from the rest of the population of a corresponding age in the following ways: Among the sick-listed were to be found more women, more persons of 50 years and over, more working-class people, and more unemployed people than in the rest of the population. Some changes have occurred between 1991-1992 and 1993-1994, of which the most important is that the share of unemployed have increased dramatically. The share of women and persons over 50 have also increased to a certain extent.

The coordinating role of the social insurance organization means for example that it shall collect information from different sources in order to estimate whether the sick person will be able to go back to work without further measures taken, or if he is in need of rehabilitation, and if disability pension will become possible. Medical background as given by the physician, and contact with the sick person are two important sources of information.

Table   A comparison between two periods, 1986-1991 and 1991-1994, regarding the share of long-term sick-listings which have had contact with the social insurance organization and occupationally oriented rehabilitation, respectively. The table also shows the number of days from the beginning of the sick period to the first contact and the first rehabilitation measure.

	1986-1991		1991-1994	
	Share	No of days	Share	No of days
Contact	31	100	60	66
Occupationally oriented rehabilitation	10	242	17	149

The results show that the social insurance organization now initiates contact in a markedly higher number of cases than before. As shown in the table, contact was initiated in 60% of the cases during 1991-1994, which is to be compared with 31% during the years 1986-1991. Contact was also initiated earlier than before; after 66 days on the sick-list in 1991-1994 compared to 100 days in 1986-1991.

Medical information was collected in 78% of the cases during 1993 and 1994, and in 73% between 1991 and 1992. A comparison between the early assessment of a case by the social insurance organization and the actual outcome shows a high degree of concordance implying that the office already at an early stage had a reasonably clear idea of what the development of the case was going to be like.

Another important source of information is the rehabilitation inquiry. Since 1992, the employer has an obligation to investigate the need for rehabilitation eight weeks after the sick-listing at the latest, unless it is obviously unnecessary. It has been discussed to what extent the employers actually carry out these investigations. The results from 1991-1994 show that when a rehabilitation inquiry is made, it is done by the employers in 56% of the cases and by the social insurance organization on behalf of the employer in 15%.

Based on the information collected by the social insurance organization, an estimation is made of the need for rehabilitation or other measures. A combination of facts from 1991-1994 shows that the social insurance organization assessed that it was best to wait with further measures in 50% of the cases. Only 1% of these cases ended with sick-benefit or disability pension. Among other cases, however, the social insurance organization had the opinion that there might be a need for rehabilitation or a right to disability pension. This implies that the social insurance organization has succeeded in drawing a clear boundary between the cases needing special attention and the ones where it is possible to await future progress.

The social insurance organization has steadily increased the share of cases undergoing occupationally oriented rehabilitation. As shown in the table, 17% of the cases underwent such rehabilitation during the period 1991-1994, as compared to 10% during 1986-1991. The measures were also taken earlier; after 149 days on the sick-list compared to 242 days in the earlier period.

Of the cases undergoing rehabilitation, 22% ended up with sick-benefits or disability pensions in the 1991-1994 period. The same group in 1986-1991 constituted 29%. This could imply that the social insurance organization has become more accurate in taking rehabilitation measures that lead to a clean bill of health. As for the final outcome of all cases, the trend is almost the opposite. During 1991-1994, 19% of the cases ended up with sick-benefit or early retirement pension, compared to 18% in 1986-1991.

Another sign of the social insurance organization having become more apt in choosing the right rehabilitation measure is that the share of persons with a relapse of their illness after starting occupationally oriented rehabilitation decreased. A comparison between 1993-1994 and 1991-1992 shows that among the cases where the social insurance organization had initiated rehabilitation, the number of persons suffering a relapse within six months after being declared fit, decreased. Among cases where no rehabilitation had been initiated or needed, there was no such change.

5 The Importance of Unemployment for Partially Disabled Workers

The study by the Swedish National Social Insurance Board: 'the Swedish National Social Insurance Board Accounts 1991:10', dealing with the importance of unemployment for certificates of good health and disability pensions, shows that the occupation of the sick-listed and the situation on the labour market in the community have a great influence on the progress of the case. Unemployed persons have longer periods of sickness and are more often represented among disability pensioners than are those who are gainfully employed. During the period that has been investigated – 1986-1991 – 6% of the long-term sick-listed were unemployed persons. In the years 1993-1994, the share of unemployed had increased to 18%. This remarkable increase must, however, be seen in proportion to the dramatic increase in open unemployment during the same period – from 2% in 1989 to 8% in 1994.

In spite of the economic prosperity and high compensation levels in sickness insurance during the studied period, there is nothing to imply that the problems caused by unemployment have decreased. Due to the lack of vacant jobs, those who have been on the sick-list for a longer period in 1991-1994 are considered to have had the same difficulties in reentering the labour market as had the same group in 1986-1991. Long-term sick-listed persons who have been unemployed during the years 1991-1994 are also expected to have had greater difficulties in reentering working life as compared to those who had employment. This pattern is supported by several studies of the situation after 1991, which all give indications that, compared to the employed, unemployed people have longer periods on the sick-list and have to wait longer before rehabilitation is initiated.

The patterns which have been noticed on an individual basis indicate that unemployment has increased the amount of compensation for lack of income due to reduced working capacity caused by sickness. This conclusion can be drawn due to the fact that unemployment has been shown to cause a decrease in the outflow from sick-lists. The total effect on the compensation volume is, however, unclear since unemployment also tends to decrease the inflow to sick-lists, which in turn may have decreased the volume of compensation.

The situation on the labour market has become somewhat brighter during 1994, and in the light of the assessment of the labour market prospects for 1995 and 1996 made by the Labour Market Board, it is possible to estimate the consequences for sick-listing and disability pension. Open unemployment is estimated to be less than 6% by the end of 1996. Unfortunately, it can be stated that, except for young persons, groups who have traditionally had difficulties with keeping up with competition in the labour market, will have a hard time in the future as well. The share of older people in the labour market will increase dramatically in the near future and, according to earlier experiences, this leads to an increased need for sick-listing and disability pensions.

The predicted occupational increase will be seen mainly in male dominated sectors whereas the female dominated part of the public sphere will decrease. There is a risk that the difficulties which many women are going to encounter will lead to an increased need for sick-listing and disability pension.

In years to come, the social insurance organization's work with occupationally oriented rehabilitation will be put to a hard test. In order to create a comprehensive view of the needs of the individual and the demands of the labour market, the social insurance organization and the labour market authorities will have to coordinate their efforts. Finally, it can be stated that there is a general tendency of increased demands for education, competence and working ability at the labour market. Under such circumstances it is a difficult task indeed to find a suitable job for a person with an impaired working capacity and insufficient education. Protected workplaces, or some other kind of sheltered employment is the only way to continued gainful employment for many persons in that situation. Unfortunately, the possibilities for such meaningful occupations are limited in the Swedish labour market of today.

6 Criticism of the Rehabilitation Work During 1991-1996

The shortage of labour during the second half of the 1980s was a strong force behind the measures that were taken in the field of rehabilitation in the early 1990s. During the period when these new rules have been in force, however, the prerequisites have differed radically from those in the late 1980s. The development has now been characterized by a serious depression, high unemployment and a marked structural change.

In spite of the difficult conditions, prevention as well as rehabilitation work have become important ways of improving the working environment, the productivity and the quality at many workplaces.

The general opinion is, however, that the intentions of the reform have had too little impact. A lot of work remains to be done before those intentions will have been fully realized.

6.1 Unclear Responsibility

Despite the fact that the plans for rehabilitation work focussed on early measures, this has not been carried through in reality. The responsibility of the employer is too vaguely formulated and the distribution of responsibility between employer and social insurance organization is unclear, not least concerning the costs.

It is also unclear when the employer is supposed to have done his duty. According to general advice from the Swedish National Social Insurance Board, the qualifications and limits for the responsibility of every employer shall be tried first when his resources are exhausted. The responsibility of the employer, as it is stated, can be interpreted in different ways, and will be so with respect to the varying points of view of the different actors.

These uncertainties about responsibility create problems and conflicts of interest as to how far it should reach and what resources the employer is supposed to supply. It can also be questioned whether the confusion about the responsibility is a driving force for early actions. It is possible that an employer – being uncertain of the consequences of it – reacts by renouncing responsibility for rehabilitation. A diffuse responsibility can hardly be considered important.

6.2 Insufficient Knowledge About Staff Economy

The focus of the employer is on his business and on production. The rational and real driving force for him to take preventive as well as adaptive and rehabilitational measures is to be able to run a business which functions as well as possible. Apart from purely humanitary benefits, the employer also has to consider these efforts as a means of keeping the business going. It means that the will and energy needed for realizing preventive and adaptive measures as well as measures of rehabilitation depends on the employer's estimation of whether it will prove beneficial for business. Aim and direction of the National Insurance Act is for the employer's responsibility for rehabilitation to be to restore the individual's capacity to work. This formulation and the employer's focus on his business can be seen as a conflict between the differing interests of the society and the employers.

Staff economy studies show, however, that measures of prevention, adaption and rehabilitation are profitable for the company. The problem is that there is a shortage of staff economy knowledge at workplace level and the possible profit of these measures is thus unclear.

6.3 Differing Chances

Different employers have different chances of fulfilling their rehabilitation responsibility.

It has not been possible to impose the same demands on all employers and expect equal results.

The group of employers is large and heterogeneous. They work under different conditions. The possibilities to take responsibility for rehabilitation therefore vary greatly. In discussions about society's support for or demands on the employers, the differing needs and possibilities of large and small companies are often pointed out. There are, however, several other differences which need to be taken into consideration. As examples can be mentioned the line of business, headmanship, the developmental state of the workplace, financial position, possibilities to take serious competence within fields such as enterprise management and staff policies, and not in the least working environment adaption and rehabilitation.

6.4 Missing a Joint Purpose

Rehabilitation is a composite conception of all such medical, psychological, social, occupationally and professionally oriented measures that will help the individual back to a normal life. The responsibility for medical rehabilitation is primarily laid on the medical health care system and that of social rehabilitation on the social services. The employer has primary responsibility for occupationally oriented rehabilitation. This also comprises professionally oriented rehabilitation, which falls mainly on labour market authorities. The role of the social insurance organization is to coordinate the entire process of rehabilitation. The most important actor, however, is the individual himself. He is responsible for actively taking part in rehabilitation and to specify his own goals and expectations.

The various measures of rehabilitation are often integrated although every authority has its own view on rehabilitation. Rehabilitation will thus depend upon different actors with varying interpretations of the word as well as on these actors' notions of the purpose of rehabilitation. Experience from the latest years points out the absence of a joint purpose for the work. Every authority has its own purpose, and they often aim in different directions, leading to conflicting priorities. Due to various reasons, the individual can sometimes not specify his own aims and expectations. The result of this is that the individual's needs are not satisfied and he falls into a border zone in between the fields of activities of the different authorities.

6.5 Imbalance in the Degree of Professionalism

If we look at the interplay between the medical health care and the social insurance, a common perspective on the concept of occupationally oriented rehabilitation is often lacking. Medical professionals have too little knowledge of the occupational possibilities for patients with different diagnoses. Epidemiological knowledge about the causes of different illnesses is not used strategically for occupationally oriented rehabilitation. Incentives have to be developed to make medical health care organizations and social insurance institutions work at this field more purposefully. There is also an imbalance between the medical health care and social insurance sectors as regards the degree of professionalism. Physicians form one of the most professional groups in society with control over their own field, special education, special forming of theories, and exercise of the profession surrounded by demands for practice, authorization and qualification. The field of occupationally oriented rehabilitation ought to develop in that direction and thus become more based on theoretical knowledge about investigation, assessment and development of the working capacity. Existing research about a 'feeling of coherence', social network and social support should also form the basis for a purposeful development within the field of occupationally oriented rehabilitation. In order to create a comprehensive view, qualified staff with competence within fields such as social work, working psychology and working science are needed. It may result in serious stress to develop a greater degree of professionalism within the field of rehabilitation. At present, the needed competence does not exist to a sufficient degree. Measures must thus be taken to create a new and more professional competence in order to be able to meet the demands concerning occupationally oriented rehabilitation. At the same time, it is important for the field of medical rehabilitation to become more influenced by questions concerning working life and judgements of working capacity.

6.6 The Risk of Being Made Redundant in Case of Superfluity

If the problem of superfluity arises, the employer often has to get rid of that part of the workforce which is old or has a low working capacity. Social insurances and collective insurances are often used strategically together with staff policies to reduce the workforce more or less voluntarily. In certain cases, there is also a risk that rehabilitation plans can form part of the 'exit strategy'. The planned measures are realized, but the employed person cannot cope with the job he is offered, therefore he gets notice to quit due to shortage of tasks, or he is asked to give a notice of resignation. It is very difficult for the authorities to apply an occupational policy in such situations. There are, however, several good reasons for the employer to invest in rehabilitation. Programmes that have been carried out show a positive effect on productivity, satisfaction in work, and presence. The conditions for this seem to be that the employers are financially and socially motivated, and that questions about working environment and rehabilitation are discussed thoroughly within the organisation.

6.7 A Lack of Preventive Measures

A lack of preventive measures in the working environment may cause ill health and redundancy of staff. During the first half of the 1990s, the Working Environment Act was changed and measures taken to strengthen the preventive work. The regulation about internal control of the working environment (AFS 1992:6) came into force on 1 January 1993. This regulation contains no demands on the employer to take any direct actions for rehabilitation. Due to this fact, the regulation is, since 1 July 1994, supplemented by a separate statement holding prescriptions about occupational adaption and rehabilitation, i.e. secondary preventive measures.

Intensified demands and a more efficient control have, however, not been sufficient to secure a wide break-through for comprehensive thinking about working environment and rehabilitation at the workplace. Insufficient knowledge of staff economy and lack of incentives are the cause of the financial benefits of prevention and rehabilitation measures not being accepted. If the financial incentives are unclear, there is no spontaneous request for information and education. It proves problematic to sufficiently spread information on internal control, occupational adaptation and rehabilitation. This is particularly true for small and middle-sized workplaces. Large companies and administrations too have highly decentralized organisations these days where the responsibility for business and profits has been delegated to several relatively small units. The regulations and systems for preventive measures as well as measures for adaption and rehabilitation must be expressed in a way that clarifies the positive financial consequences to the people responsible.

7 Unchanged Policy but Improved Conditions

In spite of the problems accounted for above, there is no reason to change the fundamental policy of today's legislation. Early, active and coordinated rehabilitation should form the basis for work also in the future. There are, however, reasons to improve and retry the conditions forming the present foundation of the measures.

This is discussed in a report, Insurance cover and sickness, SOU 1995:149, published by the Sickness and Work Injury Committee early this year. The Committee proposes a general ill health insurance based on the so-called 'work-line'. The policy today of this 'work-line' comprises the entire society, and covers several areas of politics and headmen. Its goal is for everybody to find the major part of their support through their own work.

7.1 A More Specified Responsibility for Employers in Legislation

A general ill health insurance has, according to the Committee, two important tasks to fulfil. The first is to assist efficient and preventive measures to improve the working environment, and the second to take early, active and coordinating measures of rehabilitation. The workplace is thus very important for the effect of the ill health insurance. The role and responsibility of the employer is important as regards how the activity is run and developed.

In order to specify the role of the employer at an early stage, one ought to consider measures within the following areas:

- active preparations;
- early contact with the co-workers, and identification and elucidation of the rehabilitation requirements;
- early and active measures of rehabilitation;
- contact with and information to the social insurance organization.

As discussed above, the efficiency of today's system, where the employers have four weeks at their disposal to investigate rehabilitation requirements, and eight weeks to hand over this investigation to the social insurance organization, can be questioned. The outcome of this work has not been satisfactory. The system allows too long a period before active measures of rehabilitation must be taken. If, furthermore, the practical application causes further delay, the goal of early and active rehabilitation is often not reached.

In order to achieve the direction of the employer's rehabilitation measures described above, the need of a further marking in the legislation may need to be discussed. The need for active preparations, early contact, early and active rehabilitation measures, contact with the social insurance organization, and documentation may have to be clarified in the legislation. The present demands for the employer to make a rehabilitation inquiry when an employed person has had several short-time absences or when the employee himself asks for it, should remain. However, a sharpening in the legislation can be considered concerning the employer's duties in case of sickness. The law could here be supplemented according to the ideas described above so that a fundamental rehabilitation inquiry and a documentation of the measures taken exists after four weeks at the latest.

7.2 Sanctions Against the Employer

Experience tells that the employers fail to sufficiently meet their responsibilities to make rehabilitation inquiries. The number of inquiries handed in to the social insurance organization is too low, and a lot of these are delayed and of low quality. In the debate, the social insurance organizations have therefore often demanded some kind of sanction that may be used against the employers. At present, the only possibility is for the social insurance organization to turn to the Labour Safety Inspectorate asking for measures to be taken against the employer. The Labour Safety Inspectorate has, according to the Work Environment Act, the possibility to intervene and take action against employers breaking the rules of the Work Environment Act. Within the field of rehabilitation, however, this is true only if the routines and regulations for internal control do not work, and not in the individual case of rehabilitation. To this date, the social insurance organizations have only made a few reports of this kind. The proceedings are regarded by the social insurance organization as too circumstantial and the effect of the measure as too weak. The suggestions in the debate has been to introduce some kind of sanctions directly into the General Insurance Act.

The issue of a prolonged sick-benefit period has been discussed, and several opinions have been presented, but hitherto no decision has been made. The following pros and cons have been listed:
An argument *in favour* of prolonging the sick-benefit period has been to link the responsibility for actions with the responsibility for support and thereby strengthen the employer's responsibility for early and active rehabilitation work. The aim should be for a systematic planning of the rehabilitation work to have started already within four weeks. By bringing together the employer's responsibility for actions and support in time, taking over by the social insurance organization is concentrated at one point in time. Another advantage is that this point coincides with the moment the social insurance organization shall get access to a special assurance from the insured person as well as a more detailed medical certificate. The social insurance organization will thus simultaneously receive information from the insured person, the physician and the employer. It has also been claimed that a prolonged period of sick-benefit will cause the costs for the employer to become more variable and

thereby more easy to influence. This ought to prove a strong incentive for taking action thus promoting a quicker rehabilitation process.

Arguments *against* prolonging the sick-benefit period include for example the employer's costs thereby becoming even more differentiated. This could have serious consequences for high risk enterprises, especially small ones without possibilities to spread the risks. An increased differentiation of the costs would also mean relatively more serious consequences for work intensive businesses. These are primarily dominated by women, such as social and medical health care. Sick-leave within these fields is relatively high. Arguments have also been presented that a prolonged period would constitute a risk for delaying the rehabilitation measures. The social insurance organizations would not be able to investigate the medical certificate more thoroughly nor assess the right to sick-benefit after four weeks on the sick-list. It has also been claimed that the motive only to employ persons with little chances of sick-leave will be enhanced.

7.3 Arbetsgivarinträde ('Entrance of the Employer') – an Alternative Measure

Action against employers not meeting their rehabilitation responsibility should, according to the Committee, to the greatest extent possible be based on incentives, i.e. the financial stimuli that may serve as a reason and that may be strengthened with different measures.
An alternative solution, based on financial powers, might be to let the sick-benefit period be followed by a period with *arbetsgivarinträde* ('entrance of the employer'). This means that the employer continues to give sick pay, but that this cost is later reimbursed by the social insurance organization. A prerequisite for this reimbursement would be that the repayment starts from the date the employer has met his rehabilitation responsibility. This will, however, call for a clear definition of that employer's responsibility as well as competence at the social insurance organizations to make this kind of decisions.

7.4 The Need for an Increased Coordination between Sickness Compensation and Unemployment

The unemployment insurance and present sickness insurance are two very different systems of compensation and they also serve different purposes. The rules for the estimation of income, working conditions *et cetera* differs between the systems. As a rule, a person with an income exceeding 5.5 base amounts (according to the rules valid from 1996 but with the base amount from 1995) gets a higher compensation from the sickness insurance than from the unemployment insurance.

The Committee's opinion is that compensation from an ill health insurance ought to be based only on the cash income during the first three months of sickness. This would generally mean that the sickness compensation would be lower than the compensation from the unemployment insurance, since the latter is based on other taxable income as well.

A reason for introducing limitations to the right to sick-benefit for unemployed persons is, according to the Committee, that it should not be a financial benefit for an unemployed person to be on the sick-list in stead of being at the labour market's disposal. A person who is capable of work may feel that it is unfair that a sick person should get a higher compensation. Sick-benefit being higher than unemployment compensation may also cause a flow of unemployed persons from unemployment compensation to sick-benefit. It would also be more difficult to rehabilitate a person to unemployment if he receives a higher compensation being sick.

8 Coordinated Rehabilitation for Exposed Groups

In many cases, reduced working capacity is caused by a mixture of medical, social and labour market related problems. The risks are great that individuals with such a complex of problems fall in between the nets of the various systems of compensation. Dividing into different sectors hamper a tight hold on the person's situation. Instead, every authority tries to solve the problems from their own perspective and conditions. The result is often a circle where the individual is pushed around between various authorities and different systems of compensation.

8.1 Unemployed Persons on Sick-Leave

The Governmental Committee of Sickness and Work Injury and the Committee of Labour Market Policy have established that the share of unemployed persons is much higher among persons on sick-leave than among the average population. Psychiatric diseases are also more common in the former group. The sickness periods are often longer, and it takes more time to initiate measures of rehabilitation. The risk for the sick-leave to end up in disability pension is also higher for unemployed persons. This group is estimated to count approximately 15,000 persons. The hypothesis is that a large part of this group has no firm establishment on the labour market and wanders between different supporting systems in society.

48

8.2 People with Functional Disabilities

Persons with a 'working disability' have a special register at the job offices. According to the National Labour Market Board, the number of job seekers with working disabilities has increased from a monthly average of 28,000 in 1991/92 to over 46,000 in 1994. However, the National Labour Market Board is of the opinion that the number of disabled in need of support from the Labour Exchange and the Labour Market Institute is underestimated due to the fact that a large number of persons get disability pension whereas others are not registered as disabled in spite of obvious disabilities. The difficulties on the labour market notwithstanding, the number of functionally disabled who have been given a job or other task, has remained unchanged. Every month during the financial year 1993/94, an average of 2,100 functionally disabled got a job with the help of the Labour Exchange and the Labour Market Institute. This compared to 1,600 in 1991/92.

Based on information from the National Labour Market Board, the size of the group is estimated to be around 45,000.

8.3 Young Disabled Persons

The activity of the Labour Exchange and the Labour Market Institute with special measures for young persons with functional disabilities developed through an experimental action between 1986 and 1990. The target group was persons between 16 and 29 years of age receiving sick-benefit or disability pension. The purpose was to offer competence from the Labour Exchange and the Labour Market Institute to try possibilities to work and education with the goal of totally or partly avoiding compensation via social insurance. The experimental action was conducted in close cooperation with the social insurance organizations and other rehabilitation actors. The results of the experimental action have been collected and further developed, and since 1990/91 it is part of the ordinary activities at the Labour Exchange and the Labour market Institute. The activity has increased, and so has the number of young persons with sick-benefit/disability pension taking part in it – from 1,300 in 1990/91 to 2,400 in 1994/95. During the financial year 1994/95, 53.6%, or 1,284 persons had started such activities as work, training or education.

8.4 Mentally Disabled

In the Psychiatric Commission's report (SOU 1992:72), it is established that social insurance is a very important part of the service, support and care for mentally disabled people. Mental disorders often affect people early in life. It is common that the disorders lead to severe functional disabilities which last for a long time. Many psychiatric patients therefore depend on allowances from the social service for their upkeep. Compensation under social insurance forms the major part of costs related to service, support and care for persons with chronic mental disorders. The task of the Psychiatric Commission was mainly concerned with those suffering from a chronic and severe mental illness. The Commission initiated a social study of decisions about sickness allowance or disability pension to patients with a mental disorder as their first or second diagnosis. The study involved cases in October and November 1991. Mental retardation was in this study not considered a mental illness. Every year, 7,000 to 8,000 people with a psychiatric diagnosis receive a decision about new sick-benefits or disability pensions. Mental disorders were found to be the cause of about 15% of all newly granted sick-benefits/disability pensions. 25% of the decisions concerned patients with a diagnosis of psychosis and the remaining 75% persons with the less severe forms called neurosis.

8.5 People Suffering from Psycho-social Ill Health

The concept of psycho-social ill health refers to social risk factors in the form of certain life situations and problems as well as to certain symptoms of which most are mental, but some are also somatic. The individual's conception of his situation is what comes first, and the concept can thus stand for a number of conditions and situations in a person's life.

There are studies showing that psycho-social ill health is common among patients within primary health care. In about 50% of the consultations, a pathologic cause is found, but the other half of the patients do not have objective signs of illness. In this latter group, psycho-social problems were most abundant (35%).

Studies also show that patients within primary health care with psycho-social ill health present a heterogeneous symptomatic picture with a mixture of somatic, psychological and psycho-social problems manifesting as diverse symptoms. The fact that physicians to a large extent classify the patient's problems in the form of symptomatic diagnoses may lead to the real cause being forgotten, which hampers solving the problem. It also confirms the social insurance organizations' experience that this group is very difficult to rehabilitate due to the fact that the actual reason for the patient's problems remains unclear.

9 Conclusions

As was made clear above, the question of partially disabled workers in the Swedish workforce is a difficult issue. Even though criticism has been hard as regards how few goals have actually been reached between 1991-1996 (the period during which the current legislation has been in force), it is the intention of governmental authorities to solve the problem. In Sweden, we can just hope that they will be successful.

References

SOU 1995:149   Insurance cover and sickness. A report by the Sickness and Work Injury Committee.

SOU 1992:52   A Society for All. Final report of the 1989 Commission on Policies for the Disabled.

SOU 191:46   Disability Welfare Justice. A report by the 1989 Disability Commission.

The Swedish National
Social Insurance
Board Accounts

1995:20   The National 'Long-term Sick-listing'. An investigation of long-term sick-listing and rehabilitation.

1995:10   The importance of unemployment for certificates of good health and disability pension.

1994:5   'Long-term Sick-listing' – a study of rehabilitation work by the social insurance organization.

1989:12   Long-term sick-listing, rehabilitation and disability pension. A system analysis.

The Swedish National
Social Insurance
Board Informs   Social insurance statistics. Facts from 1995.

                       Long-term sick-listing

The Unit for Social
Insurance Research

Report 1996:1   Unemployed persons on the sick-list.

Report 1995:11   The rehabilitation officers' opinion of their discretionary scope.

Report 1995:10   The development of rehabilitation within the Social Insurance.

Report 1995:9   The rehabilitation systems in Germany and Sweden.

Report 1995:5   The development of disability pension.

Report 1995:2   The physicians' sick-listing pattern.

Legal Remedies to Prevent Disability Pensioning in Norway

Asbjørn Kjønstad

1 Introduction

One of the major problems in almost all countries in Europe is that an ever increasing number of people is defined as disabled and thereby excluded from the workforce. In my home country, Norway, the first general disability pension act was put into law in 1960. Over the following 30 years the number of disability pension recipients tripled. Today almost 10% of the workforce are receiving disability pensions.

Most recipients of disability pensions in Norway are regarded as 100% disabled. Only about one-fifth of these receive a reduced pension. However, among those who have been classified as 100% disabled, there are many who have considerable remaining working ability. The reason why they nevertheless receive full disability pensions is that it has not been possible for them to utilize their remaining working abilities, and consequently obtain an income on the open labour market.

Based on this I will not limit the scope of this contribution to those who formally are regarded as partly sick, handicapped and disabled, but look at the whole group of people who are at risk of becoming or are already more or less disabled. Since this includes all of us, I will start with a model that includes the full lifespan for the population as a whole.

I will use examples from Norway since I am more familiar with the situation in my own country. However, I intend to illustrate more general problems relevant to other countries as well. The situation and many rules are quite the same in Sweden and Norway. Hence you can combine what Lotta Westerhäll writes in her article with my contribution.

2 Model for a Lifespan With or Without Disease, Handicap and Disability

Figure 1 shows a 24 cell table that may seem somewhat complicated. I will therefore first explain this model.

Figure 1. Lifetime with and without disease, handicap and disability

Normal lifetime	Supported by parents	Full-time work persons with own income					State support
Social benefits	Family allowance	None	Sick benefit	Rehabilitation benefit	Vocational benefit	Disability pension	Retirement pension
Preventive and treatment remedies	Education	Preventive measures	Medical treatment	Medical rehabilitation	Vocational training	Basic and assistance grants	Care for elderly
Situations/events	Children and youth	Risk factors	Disease	Handicap	Temporary disability	Permanent disability	Old age

The bottom row shows the current living conditions and the dangers one is exposed to. The next row from the bottom shows the remedies that the state introduces to improve the individuals functionality. The second row from the top shows subsistence benefits from the social security system. The top row shows normal life development for those who are not struck by disease, handicap or disability.

Along the horizontal axis the development over time is shown: children and young people are usually supported by their parents and obtain an education up to the age of 18 or 19 years. During this period the state contributes through family allowances and tax deductions (for dependants). Students are granted loans and scholarships from The State Educational Loan Funds while pursuing higher education.

After the educational period is over, most people start full-time work and obtain their own income. This is reflected in the figure by an arrow along the second vertical line. It rises to the top middle cell, which includes those with full-time work and their own income to cover subsistence expenses. Most people stay in this group until they retire and then receive retirement pensions, which in Norway can be considered a state support system.

Cell two in the bottom row shows risk factors one is exposed to in the labour market and life in general. The state acts in many ways to prevent risk factors leading to injury, disease or disability. I mention legislation regulating work environment, traffic regulations, preventive health care, child welfare, precautions against alcohol, illegal drugs, tobacco *et cetera*. Almost everyone tends to agree that preventive measures are very important, yet far too little is done in this field.

The second arrow points down and shows how the individual can descend from work occupation to disease. The bottom horizontal row shows that the disease can develop into handicap, temporary disability or even permanent disability. This usually lasts into old age.

This is not a preferred development. Therefore the state aims to halt it by the following remedies reflected in the second row from the bottom.

1. Medical treatment in hospitals and other health services outside of institutions.
2. Medical rehabilitation and retraining to improve physical and psychological abilities, for instance through physical therapy and technical equipment.
3. Vocational training to improve the individual's skills in the workplace, for instance through company retraining in accordance with the labour law.
4. Basic grant and assistance benefits to cover special expenses accrued from permanent disability; for instance the expenses of a special vehicle for the handicapped.
5. Home assistance, home health care, stay in retirement and nursing homes and other forms of care for the elderly and handicapped.

All such initiatives are naturally very important to prevent a development towards permanent disability so that the individual can function with a handicap and/or to make it easier for the individual to live with a handicap. Norway has expanded its public support during the whole of the post war period. This has, however, not been enough to help all sick, handicapped and disabled people to achieve maximum functionality.

In addition to these special remedies the National Insurance Scheme grants cash benefits to provide the individual with money for food, clothing, rent and other subsistence expenses. In this category we find:

1. sick-benefits for work disability due to illness, payable for up to one year;
2. rehabilitation benefits, if the individual still is work disabled and undergoes active treatment with the prospect of improving working ability, payable for up to one year;
3. vocational benefits while going through vocational training; a stage which may last from a few months up to several years;
4. disability pensions in cases of permanent disability of at least 50%, payable until retirement age is reached and
5. retirement pensions.

In the following I will look at the subsistence benefits in work disability cases due to illness paid by the National Insurance System. Specifically I will deal with the restrictions that have been enacted in the Nineties to control the growth of social security recipients. The development in these benefits are connected to the development of programmes for other marginal groups – young unskilled, older workers, the long-term unemployed, housewives and others – but there is insufficient space to discuss these connections here.

3 Sick-Benefits

Fundamental reforms were introduced in the Norwegian sick-benefits system 20 years ago. For workers, four new principles were enacted:
1. the compensation level was raised from approximately 50% to 100% coverage for lost income;
2. prior to the reform, the employees received no sick-benefits the first three days of sick leave. Now sick-benefits are granted from the first day of sickness;
3. prior to the reform, a medical certificate was required to receive sick-benefits. After the reform, benefits can be granted for the first three days based on a self

declaration from the employee to the employer where the employee evaluates his or her own ability to work;
4. prior to the reform, sick-benefits were paid exclusively through the public social security system. After the reform, the employer pays sick-benefits to his employees over the first two weeks. This is called the employer period.

The basic requirement for sick-benefits is one's inability to work due to illness.
1. In the first stages of illness, the term illness is given a broad interpretation. The fundamental prerequisite is that one has the symptoms of a disease. It is not required that the illness is diagnosed with a high grade of certainty. The employee who wakes up with dizziness and a headache, may usually inform the employer that he or she will be absent from work due to illness, without paying attention to which diagnosis might be the right one. The same applies when the general practitioner issues a medical certificate after the first three self declared days. After some days or weeks, however, physicians must find a cause for the symptoms and state a diagnosis.
2. To get sick-benefits the illness must result in work disability. The disability requirement differs between the first stage of the sickness period and the later stages. When a worker becomes ill, it is sufficient that he or she cannot perform the work the individual has at the time. However, after some days or weeks, one must change from this vocational disability evaluation to an economic one. At this later stage, one must consider whether the worker is able to perform other income related work.

The characteristics of the sick-benefits system which I have mentioned – 100% coverage for loss of income from the first day of symptoms of sickness, based on self declaration from the employee that her or she cannot perform the actual work – make the change from paid employee to social security recipient relatively 'painless'. This is a factor in the increasing number of sick-benefits recipients and the considerable increase in expenditure during the 1980s. When one has entered the role of social security recipient, it is not easy to vacate this role. Therefore, the requirements to obtain sick-benefits may influence social security payments that come after the sick-benefits period, specifically rehabilitation benefits, vocational benefits and disability pensions.

To reduce the availability of sick-benefits some important limitations have been enacted over the last few years.
1. The term illness has been restricted. The Act now explicitly states that financial and social problems do not entitle a person to sick-benefits. These problems

57

include conflicts in the workplace, monotonous and boring work, bankruptcy, life crises, divorce, death in the family, other family problems, unsatisfactory living conditions, long journeys to and from work *et cetera*.

2. The causation requirement between illness and work disability has been tightened. It now has to be 'clear' that work disability is due to illness. If, for instance, an employee has a nervous problem after a divorce, it will usually not be 'clear' that inability to work is due to 'sickness'.

3. A requirement for a special medical certificate has been introduced to receive sick-benefits exceeding eight weeks. The physician has to evaluate the possibilities for persons to become fully able-bodied again and to account for further treatment. The purpose is to ensure a quick follow up in preparation for rehabilitation and return to work life, if possible. The aim is to help a maximum number of people from a passive life as social security recipients to an active working life.

4. A rule has been passed which limits sick-benefits to twelve weeks for those who are occupationally, but not economically disabled. In this period the individual must be registered with the employment office. The purpose is to get the person from a passive existence back into the workforce.

Legislative changes played a major role in reducing the amount of cash benefits paid out for sickness in the early 1990s. However, over the last two years there has again been an increase.

1. The National Labour Union in Norway, which is the country's biggest organization for employees, and the National Trade/Business Organisation, which is the countries largest organization for employers, has for several years had a voluntary agreement of cooperation to reduce work absence due to illness. This agreement contributed to a decrease in absence due to illness in the early 1990s and to only a moderate increase during the last two years.

2. It has been proposed to reduce the sick-benefits level from 100 to 90 or 80 per cent and to introduce a one or two day waiting period without sick-benefits, but both proposals have been halted. The fact that voluntary cooperation seems to have given positive results, has been a forceful argument against legislative measures in an area workers regard as especially important – 'a holy cow', one might say – to them.

3. The government recently proposed that the employer period – when the employers pay sick-benefits – shall be extended from two to three weeks. The motivation behind a longer employer period has been to encourage the employers to establish preventive measures to reduce absence from work due to illness or disease and an early follow-up of those on sick-leave. The employers opposed

this proposal, but an enlargement of the employer period from 14 to 16 days passed by the Norwegian Parliament in December 1997.

4 Rehabilitation Benefits

Sick-benefits can only be granted for one year. To a person who is still work disabled due to illness, rehabilitation benefits may be granted. The rehabilitation benefit has to a great extent been functioning as a prolonged sick-benefits period. One limitation is – that in the transfer from sick-benefits to rehabilitation benefits – the compensation level is reduced from 100% to approximately 60% of lost income.

Previously, many could receive rehabilitation benefits for years without improving their vocational abilities. It was not even a duty to make a serious attempt to improve ones vocational abilities. Three years ago two important legislative changes were introduced.

1. One requirement that was enacted, that handicapped individuals should go through active treatment, aimed at improving working capacity. Now it is no longer enough that the person is in touch with a physician, psychologist, physical therapist and/or other health worker, but one has to undergo *active* treatment.
2. Secondly, rehabilitation benefits can now as a main rule only be granted for one year. Thus, the individual has a strong motive to reenter the workforce as soon as possible, or begin more active rehabilitation or vocational training.

These changes have resulted in a 50 per cent decrease in the number of recipients of rehabilitation benefits over a three year period. Some of those who used to receive rehabilitation benefits are now back at work or undergoing active vocational training. This is, of course, a positive sign. But many too have become recipients of disability pensions, social welfare payments or are supported by a spouse or other family members.

5 Vocational Benefits

Vocational training may start after one year of sick-benefits and one year of rehabilitation benefits, but may begin earlier. Through vocational training one seeks to build on, take advantage of and develop further the resources that the handicapped individual still retains. The aim is to get the individual back to work as soon as possible.

59

It is a requirement for obtaining vocational training benefits that the handicapped should actually participate in vocational training. The individual may receive vocational rehabilitation or training at a social medical department in a hospital, employment institute, rehabilitation centre, regular school, university *et cetera*. There are no time limits in the Social Security Act for how long vocational training benefits may be granted. In other words: one may use the time that is necessary and appropriate to improve working skills.

The amount of vocational benefit is usually the same as for rehabilitation benefits and disability pensions. Therefore, transfers between these three benefit systems are neither hindrance nor encouragement to shift over from one to another.

6 Disability Pensions

To qualify for disability pensions three main conditions have to be fulfilled:
1. a person has to have a disease, injury or defect;
2. he or she has to undergo appropriate medical treatment and vocational training. This is a condition to get a disability pension, and therefore an obligation. Above, I have dealt with sick-benefits, rehabilitation and vocation benefits as rights for the individual;
3. he or she must have the income potential permanently reduced by at least 50% due to disease, injury or defect.

Over the first 30 years after Norway introduced its disability pension act in 1960, few legislative changes were made. Legal developments derived mainly from administrative precedences. Requirements were constantly lowered, and this contributed to a strong growth in the number of disability recipients we had up to the beginning of the 1990s. Other causes for this development may be mentioned:
- greater emphasis on efficiency in workplaces;
- structural changes in the business community;
- large scale unemployment;
- an insufficient rehabilitation and vocational training system;
- more women working both at home and away from home, and
- higher pensions (more people have built up a considerable income-related supplementary pension, resulting in less difference between disability pensions and salary or wages).

Some important consequences of the increasing number of disability pensioners were, that more and more people were permanently placed outside the workforce, and that national insurance expenditure increased considerably. The government stated in 1991 that a continued 'strong increase in the number of disabled persons would weaken production options and economic growth, something that could create a distribution conflict between recipients and those actively working ... *The rapid increase in the number of recipients of disability pension is especially worrisome.*'

To limit the number of disability recipients, 20 important legal changes were made in the 1990s. I will mention some of these changes here.

1. The definition of illness, which earlier included many diffuse illnesses, was restricted.
2. A new requirement was that the illness must be the 'main cause' for the disability; until then it had been sufficient that the illness had contributed to the loss of income.
3. Stricter requirements for rehabilitation and vocational training were demanded for persons under the age of 35 with drug and alcohol addictions and other psycho-social problems.
4. Stricter requirements for geographic mobility were introduced. Norway is a country with a widely scattered population. Many handicapped people cannot obtain work in the rural areas where they live, and formerly they were usually not required to move to other parts of the country where work was available.
5. Stricter requirements for vocational mobility were also introduced. Before then a handicapped person was only expected to accept 'suitable work'; now he or she has a duty to accept 'any kind of work' he or she is able to perform.
6. The pension level was lowered, thus increasing the difference between income and pension and making it more beneficial to work.
7. Stricter sanctions were introduced for physicians with irregular practices relating to the issuing of medical reports in disability cases. This also applies in cases of sick-benefits, rehabilitation benefits and vocational benefits.

For the first 30 years, the disability pension system was rarely a subject of legislative change, and legal developments mostly came via decisions of the Social Security Tribunal and by general administrative circulars. In the 1990s government and parliament have sought to control developments in this area through legislative changes and mandates to the Ministry to pass by-laws. The disabled workers' rights have been limited, and we have had a reduction in the number of new disability recipients from 1990 onwards.

Over the two last years, however, we have again experienced an increase in the number of disability pension recipients. This is especially due to the new limitations of rehabilitation benefits (see 4, above).

The Norwegian Parliament passed a totally new National Insurance Act in February 1997. It provides three new remedies to make it easier for the disabled to combine work and pension. The goal is to ease the utilization of remaining working ability without losing the economic safety of a disability pension.

1. Previously a recipient of a full disability pension could earn approximately 10% of an average industrial worker (1/2 basic amount) without suffering a reduction in pension. The new Act doubles the allowable amount (to 1/1 basic amount).
2. Previously a disability pension recipient did not have to reapply for pension if he or she started working and the work attempt failed within one year. The new Act extends this period to three years. It is more encouraging to start work if one need not fear a repeat of the administrative process if the work attempt fails.
3. A 50% reduction of the ability to earn an income is required in order to be granted a disability pension. According to the new Act a lower percentage reduction in the income ability can entitle a person to a pension, providing a combination of work and pension is established.

7 The Companies' Responsibility for Sick, Handicapped and Disabled Persons

In Norway it is primarily the welfare state – represented by the health services, the educational system, the employment offices and the National Insurance System – which is responsible for the ill, handicapped and disabled. Families and companies have a limited legal obligation to these people.

An employer is free to decide who he or she wishes to hire. Naturally, ill, handicapped and disabled people have a harder time than others in finding work. We do not, like Germany, require big companies to hire a certain number of handicapped persons. Nor do we have a disability discrimination act or like rules as do most of the Anglo-American law countries. However, we do have incentive programmes with wage cost subsidies for public and private employers that employ handicapped people.

An employee who is frequently absent due to illness, is a financial burden for a company. As mentioned in section 3 above, the employer is required to pay sick-benefits the first 16 days during sick-leave – the employer period. The requirement of an employer period aims to motivate the employer to establish a work environment which will prevent absence due to illness.

We have a separate set of regulations for employees with chronic or extended illnesses where the risk of being absent due to illness is high. More than 35 days of sick-leave over a one year period is considered high. The employer or employee may apply for exemption from the employer period. If exemption is granted, the National

Insurance will cover all sick-benefits for the employer. This rule makes it easier for handicapped persons to get and keep work.

An employer has a certain responsibility to take care of an employee who has been vocationally handicapped due to accident, illness, injury *et cetera*. According to the Working Environment Act, an employer has a duty to take the necessary actions to make it possible for an employee to maintain their employment within the company. However, the duty to arrange internal vocational rehabilitation for vocationally handicapped, only applies 'to the extent this is possible'.

In Norway employees are quite well protected against termination of their work contract. An employer needs a 'reasonable cause' to terminate such a contract. The important question then is: do illness, handicap or disability qualify as reasonable causes? The Working Environment Act states that an employee who has been absent from work due to illness, cannot be discharged for the first six months after becoming disabled. After this period, an employment contract may be terminated as a rule, provided the employee is still unable to work.

The existence of the National Insurance System now makes it easier than before for an employer to terminate employment contracts. We have many examples of companies seeking to reduce their workforce, who peruse the medical records of their staff to find any employees with a record of illnesses as well as those who have the option of receiving rehabilitation benefits, occupation benefits and/or disability pensions. The social responsibility that many companies had for their employees in earlier days, has to a great extent been replaced with 'modern insurance abuse'.

8 Some Final Remarks

The development of the Norwegian Social Security system started at the end of the last century – inspired by Bismark's social security laws. After the Second World War the inspiration came not from Germany, but from Great Britain – the Beveridge Plan of 1942. In the mid-1960s the Scandinavian social welfare model was developed, with especially high levels of national insurance benefits.

The first hundred years of development mostly led to an expansion of benefits. Steadily new insurance schemes were introduced, requirements were lowered, and the level of benefits increased considerably.

The 1990s saw a clear change in course with several restrictions being imposed. There have been no new restrictions to entering the sick-benefits system; the restrictions are connected with the later stages. The purpose of these restrictions was first and foremost to lower the considerable cost increase and also to consider warning signs that so many were placed outside the workforce. Finally, we got the work-line policy.

The National Insurance System has mainly developed from ideologies about humanity and solidarity. As was mentioned, the restriction of the 1990s were motivated by saving money and a desire to build up the work approach – the work-line policy – instead of the social insurance approach. It is beneficial to get people into the workforce. But as many sick, handicapped and disabled people are placed outside of the insurance system, we will experience limitations in both moral and human terms.

Integration of Persons with Disabilities into the Labour Market and State Intervention: Crucial Design Features and the Effectiveness of Compulsory Employment Policy from a German Perspective

Albrecht Winkler

1 Introduction

The German *Schwerbehindertengesetz* (Severely Disabled Persons Act) as the legal basis of vocational rehabilitation and integration often serves other countries as a model for successful state intervention. Indeed it comprises an elaborate set of provisions, incentives and supportive instruments which is, in the field of labour market policy, complemented by the provisions of the *Arbeitsförderungsgesetz* (Labour Promotion Act). A strong emphasis placed on vocational training measures on the one hand and a preference for compulsory provisions on the other hand are the main features of the current German rehabilitation system. With about 860,000 disabled persons being employed (as defined by the law) it seems to be quite successful in ensuring the (continuing) employment of many disabled workers. Nevertheless, as the labour market figures reveal, its ability to (re-)integrate disabled 'outsiders' of the labour market, specifically the unemployed, is limited and the discrepancy between legal goals and actual results increases. Therefore before entering the discussion of an *optimal* policy design to close this gap, first of all the *actual* design features of the German rehabilitation system and the consequences for the labour market situation of the disabled will be considered. Limited (re-)employment chances seem to be the core problem and the main policy challenge as they indicate a limited effectiveness of legal intervention and the need for a thorough reform.

2 The Rehabilitation Process: Function and Institutions

For our purposes it is useful to distinguish measures *preparing* disabled persons for work from methods and incentives to finally *place* them in the regular labour market when they are actually 'job-ready' and training measures are completed.

In general, the concept of rehabilitation comprises all measures that enable disabled persons to participate in social and economic life equally with the help of medical treatment (medical rehabilitation), social assistance (social rehabilitation) and work-related training measures (vocational rehabilitation). Concentrating on vocational rehabilitation, the following institutions can be distinguished, which deal with different stages in the rehabilitation process and therefore different target groups:

– *Berufsbildungswerke* (Vocational Training Centres) are responsible for the initial vocational training of young persons with disabilities (esp. learning disabilities) after completion of school and before entering the labour market;

– *Berufsförderungswerke* (Vocational Rehabilitation Centres) carry out further training and retraining and are mainly directed at adults with work experience who, because of accident, injury and disability, need a vocational reorientation. The main goal of the 28 existing institutions with about 16,000 places is to restore or preserve the competitiveness of the disabled in the labour market (Mühlum 1996: 37);

– *Sheltered workshops* provide employment opportunities for those disabled persons who are not or not yet prepared for the competitive labour market. In the first case, when integration in the open labour market seems impossible, they offer long-term employment while taking care of the specific impairment in the work process and therefore serve as a *goal* of integration. In the second case, they represent an *instrument* of integration offering special training and rehabilitation measures with the aim of eventually placing those 'high-performance' employees in the open labour market. Considering that there are 590 existing sheltered workshops taking care of more than 140,000 (mainly mentally) handicapped persons,[1] they play an important role in providing job opportunities and rehabilitation measures to severely disabled people. Nevertheless, the transition to regular employment proves to be difficult as only about one out of a hundred workers can finally be placed in the open labour market. This can be explained by the interest of the sheltered workshops to retain their key workers, the lack of adequate instruments and institutions to ease the transition and the reluctance of many employers to recruit persons with disabilities despite the various (financial) incentives provided by the state.

The limited readiness to take on disabled persons is also a major impediment for the success of those institutions which stand at the end of the rehabilitation process and which have the function of placing the disabled in the competitive labour market. Here two major institutions must be mentioned.

The *employment offices* usually have a separate department that specialises on the placement of disabled job seekers. To foster (re-)integration, employment offices can take advantage of a whole set of financial measures. Worth mentioning are wage cost subsidies paid to employers for up to one year and 50% of the usual wages (training subsidy), for two years (integration subsidy) or up to three years and 80% of the wage costs (regular subsidy). Further instruments include subsidies for work trials and apprenticeships. Apart from arranging placements in the firms, the employment offices also take care of the assignment to and financial support of various rehabilitation measures outside the companies.

The *Hauptfürsorgestellen* also have several financial incentives at their disposal, including investment-subsidies in the case of newly created workplaces for the handicapped or workplace adaptations. Additionally they pay up to 800 DM per month to the employer in case of diminished performance of the disabled person or compensate for extraordinary expenses. Furthermore they offer subsequent assistance in the course of the employment relationship to solve arising problems and thereby to prevent dismissals. Finally, if all else fails, they are also involved in the dismissal procedure.

Both institutions are involved in the implementation of the Severely Disabled Persons Act which has as its main goal the integration of the disabled in work and society. The basic characteristics of the legal provisions will be presented in the following section with special emphasis being placed on compulsory elements.

3 The Rehabilitation Process: Legal Provisions and Coercive Measures

The German rehabilitation system is a comparatively complex system with a relatively strong emphasis on regulative measures. Its legal basis, the Severely Disabled Persons Act (Schwerbehindertengesetz) which was enacted in 1974 and amended in 1986, applies to those handicapped with a disablement of at least 50%. In special cases, when integration is particularly difficult, those with a lower but at least 30% degree of disability can equally be entitled to the protective and supportive measures provided by the law.

Concerning the legal intervention in companies' discretion in the field of employment policy, three major compulsory elements can be distinguished.

1. First of all, the legal provisions include a general obligation for employers to promote the employment of disabled persons, e.g. to consider the hiring of disabled persons in case of vacancies and to offer them adequate workplaces according to their skills and capabilities.

2. This general guideline is complemented by a concrete obligation for public and private employers with more than 15 workplaces to employ disabled workers with a share of at least 6% of their work-force (employment quota). An employer who does not fulfil this obligation has to pay a compensatory levy of 200 DM per month and per compulsory place. The revenue is used for the different supportive measures provided by the *Hauptfürsorgestellen*. The rationale for this provision is twofold. On the one hand, it sets direct incentives for integrating the handicapped in the firms, whilst on the other hand, it intends to distribute the employment costs of disabled workers equally between the companies.

3. As regards employment security, the disabled fall under special employment protection legislation. The employer's rights of contract termination is restricted insofar as a dismissal has to be approved by a public authority (*Hauptfürsorge-gestelle*) which must consider the interests of all participants involved in this procedure and, if possible, achieve an amicable agreement. Since the 1986 amendment, the special employment protection applies only after a six month (probationary) period.

Additional provisions include the entitlement to an extra five days (paid) leave and the election of representatives of the disabled workers in companies with at least five handicapped employees, whose duties, among others, are to foster the integration of external disabled persons.

4 Evaluating the Effectiveness of Legal Intervention: Empirical Evidence

The compulsory elements in the Severely Disabled People Act of course do not stand alone but they explicitly include a target (employment quota of six per cent) which can serve as a yardstick of comparison. Therefore it is justified at this point to take a closer look at the actual employment situation of the handicapped. Furthermore, the coercive measures represent the core of state intervention concerning the rehabilitation of the disabled in regular employment with the greatest impact on the autonomy of the companies.

The effectiveness of the quota system turns out to be limited. This can be seen directly by comparing the legal and the actual employment quota (table 1).

Table 1. Severely disabled workers employed under the quota scheme, Germany

Year	Unfilled workplaces		Actual employment quota (in %)		Private	Public
	West	Total	West	Total		
1983	232 336		5.7		5.4	6.5
1984	264 958		5.3		5.0	6.2
1985	244 646		5.0		4.7	5.9
1986	266 299		5.2		4.8	6.1
1987	287 154		5.0		4.7	5.9
1988	305 081		4.9		4.6	5.8
1989	323 902		4.8		4.3	6.0
1990	361 400		4.5		4.1	5.7
1991	398 786	475 285	4.4	4.4	4.0	5.3
1992	406 693	478 110	4.4	4.3	3.9	5.2
1993	400 367	472 203	4.3	4.2	3.8	5.2
1994	397 704	505 091	4.3	4.0	3.6	5.2

Source: ANBA, Statistik nach dem Anzeigeverfahren nach dem Schwerbehindertengesetz, Oktoberwerte, various years.

The figures even show a (more or less steady) decline in compliance with the legal provisions. In 1994, only four per cent of the relevant work places were actually filled with disabled employees. Private employers are even more reluctant to take on disabled workers shown by an actual employment quota of only 3.6%. Consequently, until 1994 the number of unfilled workplaces show a steady increase to almost 400,000 places in the western part of Germany and to more than 500,000 places for the whole country. It is important to note, however, that a complete fulfilment of the quota is hardly possible, since the number of unfilled workplaces exceeds the number of disabled job seekers.

In 1995, about 155,000 persons with disabilities (Germany West) have (officially) been unemployed. This corresponds to an unemployment rate of almost 16% which is more than six per cent higher than the general unemployment rate. The figures show a gradual increase of this gap over time indicating a worsening not only of the *absolute* but also the *relative* labour market position of the disabled (table 2).[2]

Table 2. Unemployment rate, Germany (West)

Year	Unemployment rate (total)	Unemployment rate (disabled)	Difference
1983	9.1	11.7	+ 2.6
1984	9.1	12.5	+ 3.4
1985	9.3	12.4	+ 3.1
1986	9.0	11.9	+ 2.9
1987	8.9	12.9	+ 4.0
1988	8.7	13.2	+ 4.5
1989	7.9	12.9	+ 5.0
1990	7.2	11.7	+ 4.5
1991	6.3	11.4	+ 4.9
1992	6.6	12.1	+ 5.5
1993	8.2	14.1	+ 5.9
1994	9.2	14.9	+ 5.7
1995	9.4	15.8	+ 6.4

Source: ANBA 05/91, p. 451, 751; Arbeitsmarkt 1993, p. 12; Arbeitsmarkt 1994, p. 20, Arbeitsmarkt 1995, p. 21.

Looking at the average unemployment duration for the disabled that amounts to 12.3 months (compared to 6.5 months for all) and the share of jobless disabled persons affected by long-term unemployment (table 3), every second disabled person being unemployed for more than one year (compared to 33%), the core problem becomes evident. The high unemployment rate is predominantly a result of a long duration of unemployment or low outflow rates.[3]

Table 3. Long-term unemployment, Germany (West)

Year	Share of long-term unemployed in total unemployment (in %)		Average duration of unemployment (in months)	
	total	severely disabled persons	total	severely disabled persons
1985	31.0	52.8	6.8	12.0
1990	29.7	50.8	6.7	12.4
1991	28.3	49.5	6.7	12.2
1992	26.6	46.3	5.7	13.4
1993	26.0	44.2	5.6	12.6
1994	32.5	48.5	6.5	12.3
1995	33.3	49.9		

Source: ANBA various years.

Moreover, the effectiveness of *special job security legislation* seems to be limited in periods of economic downturn. In general, employees with disabilities enjoy a higher job stability reflecting the rationale of internal labour markets on the one hand and the existence of legal norms on the other hand. However, the provisions have no employment securing effects in case of plant closures *et cetera*. Indeed, the inflow into unemployment indicates a slight erosion of job security in recent years with the disabled having a 3.7% share of the inflow compared to a 3% share of the work-force. As can be shown by the (rising) number of applications for dismissals to the *Hauptfürsorgestellen*,[4] most dismissals have been approved (with or without the consent of the disabled) or were to an increasing extent due to plant closures. It is hard to estimate, however, how many dismissals have been prevented by the procedure laid down in the act.

5 The Pitfalls of Legal Intervention

In analysing the pitfalls of current legal intervention, a micro-economic perspective has been shown to be promising. In general the firm's employment behaviour and the selection among different alternatives, which are to be influenced in favour of the disabled, is predominantly determined by cost considerations.

71

The current system of compulsory employment and compensatory levy basically leaves the companies with three different options (Sadowski *et al.* 1992):
– firms can pay the compensatory levy instead of hiring disabled persons. *De jure*, this payment does not release companies from the obligation, *de facto* it does;
– they can continue the employment of long serving employees who become disabled in the course of their employment in the firm and to strive for an official recognition of their disability status (internal recruitment or self-recruitment);
– they can hire persons with disabilities from the external labour market to meet the legal requirements (external recruitment).

In many cases it can be expected that companies prefer the first two solutions because the compensation payment is in general too low compared to the objective employment costs (extra leave, dismissal costs, perhaps lower productivity) and subjective employment costs (higher perceived employment risk, presumed lower productivity). The second option has the advantage not only of fulfilling the legal obligation (at least partly), but also of meeting the expectations of the staff in terms of loyalty and fair treatment. Additionally, the employer can be certain about the skills and abilities of the employee in question.

On the other hand, despite the legal provisions and generous financial subsidies for the hiring of disabled job seekers, employers are reluctant to take on disabled persons from outside. This limited willingness to hire disabled people from the external labour market is reflected in the high share of disabled who are (long-term) unemployed, placed in insurance schemes and early retirement programmes or are discouraged and withdraw from active labour market participation. These trends clearly run counter to the legal intentions of equal opportunities and comprehensive participation in the labour market and represent the main policy challenge.

This development seems to confirm those who consider any legal intervention in the labour market as harmful or at least ineffective. On the other hand it is always difficult to compare the effects of a hypothetical situation without compulsory elements with the status quo. It is, however, doubtful whether coercive measures alone are an adequate instrument to foster the rehabilitation of the handicapped in the work-force and whether the provisions are currently designed in an optimal fashion. Therefore one also has to point to the principle problems associated with legal intervention as there are unintended side-effects, loopholes and unjust distributive effects before considering alternatives.

The introduction of coercive measures in the rehabilitation system clearly follows the rationale that companies in general do not see integration of the handicapped in their work-force as a value in itself. Therefore, the employment of disabled persons must be either economically advantageous or enforced by legal norms. The existing concept of coercion and negative financial sanctions fits into this frame of thought.

In general, legal norms intervene in the individual autonomy of decision and produce costs when behaviour is actually to be modified. Here a trade-off exists between the strictness of coercive measures and the burden the companies have to bear. A major problem associated with the six per cent employment quota is that it does not adequately account for the differing capability of companies and consequently the differing costs involved in the employment of handicapped persons. Depending on branch and firm size, the actual employment quota as an indicator for this ability varies considerably. As one would expect, construction and agriculture have the lowest share of disabled people on their payroll (below 3%) and public/social administration the highest (over 5%). Additionally, the preparedness to employ the disabled increases with company size (number of employees) which may reflect better opportunities to deploy persons with disabilities effectively and provide appropriate workplaces. The indicator 'actual employment quota' is of course quite problematic, as it does not differentiate between lack of will and lack of opportunities to employ the disabled. But at least a correlation of actual share and the workplaces available for the disabled can be expected.

The lack of differentiation on the side of the disabled represents a related drawback of actual legal intervention. Admittedly, there are possibilities to count disabled workers with a specific and severe work-related impairment twice (or three times in rare cases) when calculating the compulsory places (multiple assignment). But in general, the official degree of disability does not say anything in respect to the actual degree of diminished performance in a specific workplace.[5] Again, the consequence is an uneven distribution of the (potential) burden associated with the employment of persons with disabilities depending on the extent of reduced productivity.[6]

Legal norms which are flexible, i.e. which leave firms with alternatives, certainly produce less costs and negative effects on competition. On the other hand, when the costs associated with the alternative choice (paying the compensatory levy) are set too low compared to the fulfilment of the legal obligation (hiring the handicapped), the success of the provisions will be limited. This is exactly the case in Germany. Additionally the quota system provides no incentives for an overfulfilment of the employment quota or for small firms with less than 16 employees.

Besides the limited effectiveness of legal norms there could also be unintended side effects. One example is the frequent recommendation to forgo the official recognition of the disability status because the advantages connected with the entitlement to supportive measures may be outweighed by the disadvantages due to stigmatisation and costs associated with legal 'protective' provisions. These provisions (e.g. including the entitlement to five days extra leave) are intended to favour the disabled but have been shown to have a harmful effect on employment chances as they impose extra costs on the companies and therefore may reduce the willingness to hire persons with disabilities.

These additional costs therefore increase the benefits of non-compliance with the employment quota mainly to the disadvantage of those remaining outside. Particularly the special employment protection leads to a redistribution of employment chances contributing to a further exclusion of the unemployed. Here, it is important to distinguish between the actual and perceived strictness of the provisions, the latter being crucial to the willingness to hire disabled job seekers. As the evidence has shown, dismissals are in fact possible although they are subject to a lengthy procedure with uncertain outcome and potential conflicts. But in the view of many employers these provisions imply a significant restriction and represent a major deterrent to additional employment as they increase the risk of hiring the disabled.[7]

6 Policy options

In view of the poor rehabilitation prospects of the disabled in the open labour market and the limited effectiveness of the traditional (financial) measures, one alternative approach would be to refrain from (additional) intervention into companies' employment behaviour and to ignore or even support the trend towards exclusion of the disabled from the open labour market. As the situation is aggravated by the high general unemployment and low labour demand that increases the competition on the supply side of the labour market, disillusion is widespread about the possibilities of legal intervention and chances of fundamental improvements of the present situation.

Such a strategy could either take the form of early retirement and disability pension or creation of a complementary, state funded labour market. Both instruments seem to be useful in particular cases. But in general these strategies not only place a burden on the social security system, they also counteract the goal of normalisation and participation of the disabled in social and economic life and do not adequately compensate for the disadvantages due to disability as intended by the law. Employment in a complementary or secondary labour market is certainly a better alternative to being unemployed considering the well-known damaging effects of unemployment on personality, qualification and future labour market chances. But such measures ranging from traditional job-creating schemes to 'social companies' and 'self-help firms' are not a general answer since they could produce locking-in effects and additional segregation.

If the goal to foster employment in the *regular* labour market and to modify the hiring behaviour of the firms is to be maintained there remain basically three different strategies (Semlinger 1988: 44):

— *regulative intervention* puts some pressure on the behaviour of companies (the actual degree depending on strictness) via legal obligations and sanctions;

— the strategy of (passive) *subsidisation* follows the rationale not only of compensating for the additional expenses involved in the employment of persons with disabilities (lower productivity or necessary workplace adaptations) but also of setting positive financial incentives to alter the hiring preferences in favour of the target group;

— the *service strategy* comprises transfers in kind *enabling* the firms to behave in a desired way by giving helpful instructions on *how* to employ disabled persons efficiently. This could take the form of information, counselling and technical assistance including information about the range of supportive measures available and overcoming prejudices about the disabled.

The option to tighten the law in face of the poor performance of current provisions could either imply an increase in the compulsory nature of legal provisions or higher negative sanctions in the case of non-compliance. Here, besides increasing the level of the compensatory levy, a reduction of traditional protective provisions which could harm the competitive position of the disabled people in the labour market should be considered. Both measures would bring the costs of fulfilment closer in line with the costs of choosing the alternative.[8]

But this purely economic point of view represents only one side of the coin. In general, the lack of information connected with widespread prejudices about the capability of disabled people to cope with the requirements of working life prove to be an obstacle for successful rehabilitation that leads especially smaller firms to use the supposedly easier and well-known alternative, that is to pay the levy. However, it is not only the *subjective attitude* towards the handicapped that frequently has to be modified by moral persuasion and comprehensive information. The *objective capability* to employ the handicapped has to be developed as well. This calls for an activation and extension of the *service strategy* compared to the strategy of mandatory and subsidised employment, the more so because the evidence points to relatively low utilisation and limited (net) effects of wage-cost subsidies.

Above all, more attention should be paid to the placement process and the institutions involved. Improvements in this field are regarded as being the most cost-effective approach in active labour market policy in general (Calmfors 1994) and for the rehabilitation of the handicapped in the labour market particularly. However, the current rehabilitation system does not (yet) correspond sufficiently to these requirements. The low number of (successful) job placements indeed gives cause for disillusion about the effectiveness of the public employment service in implementing the legal provisions despite the availability of wage-cost subsidies. While the disabled have a six per cent share among the unemployed, their proportion of people successfully placed amounts to only one per cent. Furthermore, many new employment contracts are terminated after a relatively short period which also indicates a insufficient 'quality' of the matching-performance.

In particular, frequent and intensive contacts between the relevant institutions (*Hauptfürsorgestelle* and employment office) and the companies and a greater attention to the situation in the firms is crucial to the chances of integration of disabled people (Sadowski *et al.* 1992: 92). However, in this study about half of the examined firms reported no contact and only six per cent reported frequent contact with the *Hauptfürsorgestelle*. Within five years, only 16% of the firms were visited by one of their representatives for information and consultation. This is, although to a lesser extent, also true for the employment offices. Here, about 44% of the firms are in contact with the administration, but only 35% report of attempts to arrange placements of at least one disabled applicant.

It is interesting to note though, that the efforts to establish contacts increase with firm size and smaller firms are often ignored. On the other hand, smaller firms are in greater need of information, consultation and persuasion as prejudices about the (unemployed) disabled are particularly widespread and deeply rooted. Thus it can be concluded that more attention should be paid to smaller firms to foster the chances of the disabled to be integrated in the labour market.

In recent years, however, new models have been introduced gradually in some areas which seem promising as they address the deficiency of current placement efforts. The so-called *Eingliederungsfachdienste* (integration specialist services) offer intensified placement services to ease the transition from sheltered workshops or from unemployment to the open labour market. Improving job-search effectiveness by individual assistance and increasing the willingness to hire disabled persons by co-operation and information are the main features. Additionally, they offer assistance and support to the companies and the employee in question during the employment period (job coaching).

7 Reducing Uncertainty in Employment Decisions

In the following, one aspect will be stressed that is often neglected in the discussion and present design of rehabilitation policy. The data presented indicate that poor reintegration prospects reflecting the employer's caution to hire the disabled pose the main problem. There is considerable evidence that risk and uncertainty play a decisive role in the hiring behaviour of the firms that often dominate pure cost-benefit aspects.

Flanagan (1988) interprets the European unemployment experience which, in contrast to the US-labour market development, is characterised by high persistence, high long-term unemployment and consequently low outflows from unemployment from a 'reluctance to hire' point of view. The reduced chance of leaving unemployment could either be a result of workers' lacking willingness to search for jobs or employers' reluctance to hire. While the first possibility can be neglected in times of excess labour supply, the second concept seems to be an appropriate explanation for the poor rehabilitation prospects of the disabled in the labour market as the presented evidence points to even lower outflow rates from unemployment for this target group.

According to this view the following factors (apart from usual labour costs) influence the decision to hire and whom to hire:
- fixed employment costs,
- uncertainty about future demand,
- uncertainty about employee quality.

The application of the 'reluctance to hire' approach to the labour market problems of the disabled seems fruitful, since they are even more affected by these factors for the following reasons: state intervention, the uncertainties connected with the health status of the disabled and prejudices of employers concerning the performance of this group.

While there are some 'natural' fixed employment costs (human capital formation) that lead to a preference for 'insiders' compared to job seekers ('outsiders') or others, that apply to all job seekers equally (general employment protection), there are some employment costs resulting from special protection legislation that alter the hiring preferences unfavourably for the handicapped. The perceived strictness of job security legislation is also linked to the (increasing) uncertainty of the economic environment as it increases the existing caution to take on new staff. Also when information about employee quality is imperfect *ex ante* a higher reluctance to hire can be expected. Presumably, job-applicants from a heterogeneous group with an (often invisible) impairment are particularly affected by the problem of uncertainty. Again the existing problems of asymmetric information and prejudice are exacerbated by special employment protection measures which increase the employment risk for firms.

All those factors not only have negative effects on the *general* willingness to hire, but also a redistributive impact on the employment chances to the disabled's disadvantage which is, as the relevant labour market figures show, not compensated by the quota system and the supportive measures that are available for both employees and employers.

If, because of the positive effects on employment stability, the special protection provisions for the handicapped should be preserved, alternative instruments that reduce the 'barriers to entry' for the disabled outsiders without putting the insiders too much at risk have to be used.

In order to lower the employment risk in case of an economic downturn or especially dissatisfaction with the employee's performance the increased use of non-binding employment forms prior to the regular employment relation could prove fruitful. This employment period could serve as a screening device and thereby reduce the uncertainty involved in the hiring process.

One approach is to increasingly use agency work (temporary work) as a labour market tool. It has proved effective for the long-term unemployed in reducing employers' doubts about their qualifications and motivation. Under some circumstances disabled job seekers too may increasingly benefit from this concept. Above all it could be suitable for those who suffer 'merely' from statistical discrimination and who are not or only slightly affected by diminished performance. As mentioned before, it is wrong to equate a high degree of disability with low productivity.[9]

The idea of using temporary work as a labour market instrument was first implemented in the Netherlands (START) in the late Seventies.[10] At present it serves as a model for the foundation of a considerable number of temporary work agencies in Germany. This approach seems to be an adequate answer not to all but to a large number of impediments to successful rehabilitation of the disabled in the labour market.

– The companies can use agency work as a screening device to reduce the uncertainty involved in the hiring process. Because all risks associated with their employment (sick- benefits, dissatisfaction with the performance, hiring and firing costs) are transferred to the agency, the chances of those unemployed persons whose recruitment is regarded as particularly risky, in terms of *supposed* low productivity, resulting from stigmatisation and statistical discrimination, can be improved.

– The agency workers themselves benefit through the accumulation of work experience and ending of the unemployment status which produces negative effects of stigmatisation and human capital depreciation.

– As the agency itself strives for intensive contacts with (potential) clients and above all tries to secure an optimal fit in placing the workers into the firms, it is able to develop a positive image which could have beneficial effects on the future employment chances of the former unemployed. This is important, because a widespread recourse to the service of a labour market intermediary is the prime precondition for a successful placement. Opposingly, the (mainly) negative image of the employment office (resulting from poor matching-quality) is a major impediment in placing the jobless disabled in companies because many do not consider applicants sent by the employment office.

By reducing the uncertainty and irreversibility of the hiring process, temporary agency work could be a first step (back) into the labour market getting the companies at least to the point of considering disabled applicants and of testing him or her. It is obvious though, that in case of diminished performance this would have to be supplemented by wage cost subsidies. But it can still make the employment decision in favour of a disabled person less risky.

8 Towards an Adequate and Consistent Policy Mix

All in all, a policy mix taking into account the diversity of the labour market problems of disabled people is most promising for successful rehabilitation into the workforce.

– As to the disabled, an extension of (re)qualification measures is necessary to increase their competitiveness in the labour market and to close the gap between workplace requirements and the personal skills of the disabled.[11] Besides the attainment of formal degrees this should include the development of social skills as well as passing on relevant knowledge to meet the requirements of the application procedure.

– With regard to the institutions involved in the rehabilitation process, the evidence points to the importance of individual and assisted placement efforts in connection with intensified personal contacts to employers and a pro-active acquisition of workplaces. Getting the worker and disabled representatives involved in this procedure and sharpening their awareness of the situation of the disabled outside the companies seems to be another promising path. Equally important is the availability of assistance for employers as well as for employees (job-coaching) after successful placement to prevent and solve problems arising during the course of the employment relation.

– Finally the reduction of informational deficits could open up additional job opportunities particularly in smaller firms. Providing additional information about the availability of supportive measures and the actual implications of the special employment security provisions, tackling widespread prejudices about the disabled in general and facilitating the screening of disabled job-applicants in particular fall under this category. Nevertheless, particularly in case of an *occupational* handicap, (wage-cost) subsidies still remain necessary.

Eventually with an improved and wider range of instruments it is possible to make use of the increasing proportion of vacancies that are reported as being suitable for the disabled (table 4).

Table 4. Vacancies for severely disabled persons, Germany (West)

Year	Vacancies for severely disabled persons (total)	Vacancies for severely disabled persons (per cent of all vacancies)
1984	9 523	10.5
1985	15 729	13.4
1986	46 335	28.0
1987	64 938	36.1
1988	81 227	39.8
1989	118 938	41.1
1990	143 286	44.8
1991	167 123	49.0
1992	165 312	52.0
1993	122 217	53.5
1994	137 804	57.1
1995	151 767	59.1

Source: ANBA: Arbeitsmarkt 1995, p. 118.

Although the figures may partly reflect a change in the registration practice for vacancies, they indicate a change in working conditions and job characteristics in favour of the disabled. This potential 'merely' has to be converted into concrete job offers for persons with disabilities. But one major impediment still remains: 46% of the unemployed disabled persons are 55 years or older. The high average age is regarded as a significant barrier to successful placement besides the disability itself and a long duration of unemployment and it limits the capability of the aforementioned placement models to foster reintegration.

The German experience shows clearly that mandatory employment connected with negative (compensatory levy) or positive subsidies (wage-cost subsidies) may be a necessary condition but by far no sufficient condition for inducing equal opportunities for disabled people. Sometimes coercive measures even prove to be an additional obstacle to successful integration as shown by the effects of special employment protection on the hiring behaviour of the firms. Instead, more emphasis should be placed on implementing the service strategy (information and counselling), improving the placement process and reducing risk and uncertainty in the hiring process.

References

Anba (Amtliche Nachrichten der Bundesanstalt für Arbeit), various years.

Anders, D., Die Werkstatt für Behinderte – der andere Weg ins Arbeitsleben, in: E. Zwierlein (Ed.), Handbuch Integration und Ausgrenzung: behinderte Menschen in der Gesellschaft, Neuwied, 1996, p. 574-562.

Brandt, F., Behinderte auf dem allgemeinen Arbeitsmarkt. Saarbrücken, 1984.

Calmfors, L., Active labour market policy and unemployment: A framework for the analysis of crucial design features (OECD Labour Market and Social Policy Occasional Paper, 15), Paris, 1994.

Flanagan, R. J., Unemployment as a hiring problem, in: OECD Economic Studies, 1988, No. 11, p. 123-154.

Knappe, E., M. Walger, Marktwirtschaftliche Elemente in der Schwerbehindertenpolitik, in: A. Iwersen, E. Tuchtfeldt, Sozialpolitik vor neuen Aufgaben, Bern, 1993, p. 421-441.

Lunt, N., P. Thornton, Employment policies for disabled people. A review of legislation and services in fifteen countries, York, 1993.

Mühlum, A., Sozialpolitische Bedeutung und Leistungsfähigkeit der Berufsförderungswerke, in: G. Vonderach, Berufliche Rehabilitation in Berufsförderungswerken, Edewecht, 1996, p. 33-45.

Sadowski, D. et al., Die Wirkungsweise des Schwerbehindertengesetzes – Vollzugsdefizite und Verbesserungsvorschläge, Trier, 1992.

Schröder, M., Betriebliche Vollzugskosten der Arbeits- und Sozialgesetzgebung. Ein internationaler und intertemporaler Vergleich, Frankfurt/New York, 1997.

Semlinger, K., Staatliche Intervention durch Dienstleistungen, Berlin, 1988.

Semlinger, K., G. Schmid, Arbeitsmarktpolitik für Behinderte, Basel, 1985.

Zentras – Zentrum für Arbeit und Soziales (Hrsg.), Dokumentationssystem Schwerbehinderte und Arbeitswelt, Teil II: Statistisches Archiv, Bd. 9, Trier, 1996.

Appendix

Table 5. Numbers of employed / unemployed disabled workers, Germany

Year	Employed disabled workers		Unemployed disabled workers
	West	Total	West
1983	1 002 292		131 160
1984	959 879		138 316
1985	917 654		136 008
1986	887 726		126 585
1987	878 373		126 802
1988	817 006		130 523
1989	809 776		126 662
1990	806 579		120 759
1991	842 290	974 857	116 764
1992	843 216	926 478	124 825
1993	810 600	895 463	144 410
1994	770 447	861 912	155 736
1995			155 459

Source: Bundesarbeitsblatt December 1979-1988, ANBA various years.

Figure 1. Actual employment quota, Germany

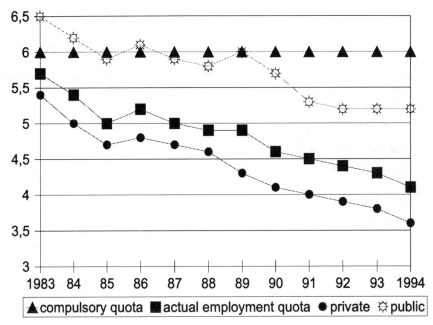

Source: ANBA, various years (Statistik ausdem Anzeigeverfahren nach dem SchwBG, Oktoberwerte)

Figure 2. Severely disabled workers under the quota scheme, Germany

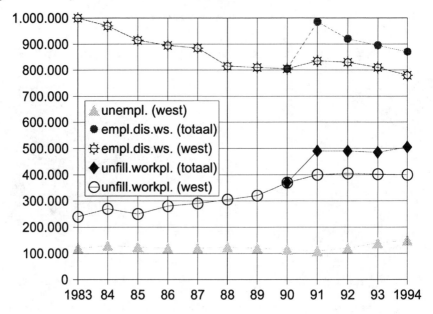

Source: ANBA, various years.

Figure 3. Unemployment rate, Germany (West)

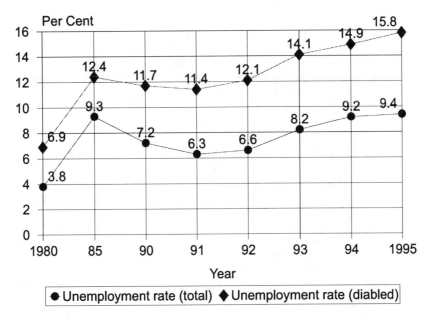

Source: ANBA various years.

85

Endnotes

1. About 80% of the disabled workers in sheltered workshops are mentally handicapped, 12% have psychological disabilities and less than 6% are affected by physical impairments (Anders, 1996, 555).

2. The official unemployment figures represent the most obvious indicator of deficient goal attainment. However, they convey only an incomplete picture of the severe labour market situation of the disabled. In particular, the withdrawal from the labour market as reflected by low labour force participation rates is ignored as well as the high proportion of disabled people placed in labour market programmes.

3. Long-term unemployment itself turns out to be an additional barrier to re-employment as it may be associated with human capital depreciation and stigmatising effects.

4. The number of applications for dismissal amounted to about 21.000 in 1986, 14.000 in 1989 and (after a steady rise) 32.000 in 1993 (Zentras 1996, Tab. 54).

5. In this context it is interesting to note that disabilities are to a great extent invisible. Among the 6.5 million persons with disabilities in Germany about one third is affected by limitations of internal organs.

6. However these costs of 'lumping everyone together' must be confronted with the costs of differentiation (enforcement and control costs) when deciding about the appropriate degree of legal differentiation (Schröder, 1997).

7. In a study more than 70% of the employers reported, that the special employment protection reduces their willingness to hire (Brandt 1984, 188).

8. To provide additional incentives also in case of overfulfilment of the employment quota and for firms with less than 16 employees a 'fund-model' has been proposed which includes a bonus for overfulfilling firms (including smaller firms) financed by the levy paid to the fund by the underfulfilling employers. Additionally, a market for employment certificates could be established to find the adequate bonus/levy-level. Then overfulfilling firms preferring the employment of the disabled could sell certificates to those which value the costs of the employment of disabled persons higher than the price for the certificate. This cost-effective mechanism with the market balancing supply and demand would ensure the fulfilment of a given employment quota and therefore contribute to goal attainment not for every company but from a macroeconomic view (Knappe, Walger, 1993, 434 ff).

9. One conclusion would be to abandon the present concept of disability (at least in the labour market area) in favour of a work-related classification that accounts for the extent of diminished performance. A different path taken by Denmark is to principally refrain from special treatment of the disabled and to solve their employment problems mainly by falling back on the general measures of active labour market policy (Lunt, Thornton, 1993).

10. Recently, START has enlarged its range of measures (e.g. by outplacement, secondment and job coaching) to account for the heterogeneity of labour market problems of the disabled and other target groups.

11. There is evidence that besides discriminatory behaviour, regional imbalances between labour supply and vacancies for the disabled do exist as well as mismatch concerning occupation and qualifications of persons with disabilities on the one hand and the requirements of the jobs on the other hand.

(Re-)Integration of People with Disabilities in View of Developments in the Belgium Labour Market

Erik Samoy

1 Introduction

A work disability may occur when a person with health problems enters the labour market. If the net result is regularly unfavourable, with the person failing to find work, losing his job or working below his potential, work disabilities develop. Governments are trying to prevent, alleviate or eliminate these by means of (re-) integration measures, aimed both at the person with the health problems and the employers, and by creating special workplaces for disabled people. Most policy evaluations only take a specific measure or a set of measures into account, neglecting the processes taking place in the labour market and their consequences for both the integration of people with disabilities at work and the relevant policies. Sometimes, consideration is given to developments in the demand for labour and the attitudes and behaviour of employers, but shifts in the nature of labour are rarely incorporated into the analysis. Where these shifts do feature is in research into the health and safety aspects of particular types of work. The findings are mainly translated into proposals for preventative measures at company level. Consequently, important shifts in the world of work and in the social definition of labour do not, as a rule, receive the attention they deserve. It is all the more remarkable since these themes actually feature in research into other problem groups in the labour market, and one school of thought among the scientific and political approaches to work disabilities blames their existence entirely on the structure of the labour market (Oliver, 1990). In this contribution, we will attempt to look at (re-)integration of disabled people in relation to developments in the labour market.

Firstly, the position of people with disabilities in the labour market is examined. Secondly, a few developments in the world of work and of the anticipated impact on disabled people are highlighted. Finally, we will look at the consequences of this for an optimal (re-)integration policy.

2 A Disability Never Comes Alone

Information about where disabled people are situated in the labour market can be found in various sources: surveys of the prevalence of disabilities (e.g. Martin, 1989; Statistics Canada, 1993), unemployment statistics (e.g. Ravaud, 1995; Frick, 1992) and studies of the state of the labour market in general (e.g. Sly, 1995), or of disabled people in particular (e.g. Prescott-Clarke, 1990). Some studies are restricted to one country (e.g. Mcneil, 1991) while others contain international comparisons (e.g. Grammenos, 1993). Although the results of these studies vary according to the country they are based on and the sources and research methods they use, they consistently show that people with disabilities – whichever way this group is defined – occupy a worse position in the labour market than people without disabilities. Disabled people are unemployed more often and for longer periods than people without disabilities. Furthermore, disabled people are less likely to be unemployed the more years of training they have had, and more likely to be unemployed as they get older. Women with disabilities have fewer opportunities in the labour market than men. In the USA, unemployment figures are higher for black or Latin-American people with disabilities than for white disabled people (see Mcneil, 1991; Christmann, 1988). The various factors are mutually reinforcing:
'Disability makes a bad situation worse, accentuating racial and age differences in labor force trends by hastening the withdrawal of older men from the labor force, especially older non-white men, and slowing the entrance of women, especially young non-white women' (Yelin, 1992: 128).
These observations are very important for the reintegration policy. For most disabled people, the disability is not the only and sometimes not even the most important 'personal' factor influencing their poor status in the labour market.
The strong and consistent correlation between 'personal' factors and job opportunities is in itself only a statistical link which is established *a posteriori*. The question is how this link occurs. The way a particular group succeeds in the labour market depends on the attitudes and behaviour of the members of that group, of potential employers, and possibly also of intermediary bodies such as employment agencies or informal referral agents. The relevance of personal factors such as age, sex, education, race and ability depend on how they are perceived by all parties involved, and the way this influences their behaviour. Employers include the disability factor in a kind of cost-efficiency calculation. They consider not only whether a disabled job seeker meets the technical job requirements, but also, for instance, the consequences of his employment for social relations in the workplace. Stereotypical attitudes regarding what a disabled person may 'only' be able to do play a larger role with new recruits than when an employee becomes disabled while in work, because

the employer will have more relevant information in the latter case. From interviews with employers, it appears that their judgement of the abilities of a disabled person are strongly influenced by the nature and seriousness of the disability (e.g. Dench, 1996; Brandt, 1985). These perceptions are, on the whole, shared by both the disabled people themselves and by employment agencies – particularly non-specialist ones – putting a damper on the effort made to find work. The same applies to other factors which are badly rated in the labour market, like a lack of skills or advanced age.

When applying for and obtaining employment, the special social status of people with disabilities in the welfare state also plays an important part. After all, they have the option, when their disability is sufficiently serious, to abstain or withdraw from the labour market, and to live on benefits. The qualifying conditions for benefit allocation and the actual benefit rates will determine whether and to what extent disabled people will look for employment, and whether employers and employment agencies would wish to consider them for jobs. Anyway, a disability is not the only factor which puts people in this position. In recent years, older employees have been given many opportunities to opt out of employment. Since the occurrence of disabilities increases with age, many disabled people are consequently eliminated from the employment process.

Policy makers and scientists have been trying to find out why there has been a steep increase in the number of people incapable of working and entitled to disability benefits in the industrialised countries (e.g. Stone, 1984; Hibbeln & Velema, 1993; Berthoud, 1995). The underlying reasons given relate to those incapable of working, the benefit system and the way it operates; namely: the ageing of the working population and the associated increasing morbidity, the level of the benefits and the calculating behaviour of potential recipients, the flexibility of the disability category, the laxity of the gatekeepers, and the fact that the latter's judgements are hard for the government to control.

Understanding the underlying causes for work disabilities and their increasing incidence is obviously also important for (re-)integration. The issue of (re-)integration is usually approached as a search for ways of either making the corrective measures more efficient or the resorting to benefits less appealing. However, incapacity for work is only a relative notion, indicating a discrepancy between the capacity of a job seeker and the needs and requirements of the labour market. Developments in the labour market – including not only the relationship between supply and demand and the distribution of demand over the various economic sectors, but also changes in the production processes of goods and services – do not receive the same scrutiny from policy analysts. Yelin is an exception to the traditional approach, with his attempt 'to demonstrate that the structure of work and employment is the proper focus for work disability policy and to redirect attention away from the unresolvable and pointless debate as to whether medical need or personal choice to withdraw from work is responsible for work disability' (Yelin, 1992: 15). He demonstrated 'that persons with disabilities are the wrong kind of leading edge, being the first fired from industries shedding workers and the last hired in ascending ones' (Yelin, 1992: 151). Disabled people and more particularly, the older, partially disabled (male) employees disappear first from withering industrial branches and near-extinct professions. They are last in line to benefit from new services, particularly in the commercial sector, which employ mostly women. The rise in employment of disabled women is much less pronounced, though, than that of able-bodied women.

3 The Future of the Labour Market

When the nature and the organisation of work are at least as important for the existence and development of work disabilities as the limits imposed by health, perceptions, attitudes and behaviour of the various parties involved and the characteristics of the benefit system, they are equally important to the (re-)integration policies. The nature of the work is not changing in a uniform way. Various intermingling trends can be found, with unpredictable consequences for disabled people. We will nevertheless try to highlight a few examples of change.

One approach to examining the work circuit is to look at the (no longer that) new technologies. Rendenbach (1990: 57-58) outlines a few developments, and the potential repercussions for both the generation of health problems, and the employment opportunities for disabled people.

1. Through the introduction of new technologies, some health-threatening production methods are disappearing, namely heavy and dangerous labour. In particular, physical disabilities caused by the production process are occurring less frequently. New production methods, however, also entail new forms of work stress which can lead to mental problems.

2. Both in industry and in the service sector, new technologies lead to automation and rationalisation. As a result, a number of unskilled jobs are disappearing. The 'niches' in companies which used to offer a haven for partially disabled employees are disappearing.

3. Technical innovations are creating new jobs for highly trained disabled people. The introduction of computers has given a number of physically disabled people a new opportunity. Less well skilled disabled people, among which are people with mental disabilities, are only given opportunities when the intellectual job require-

ments are not too high, and when the work is mostly routine. The latter still happens, but data processing is currently often carried out in other parts of the world, also because data transmission does not pose any problems.

4. Continuous technological innovations in the production process require employees to undergo in-service training (life-long learning). This can cause particular problems for people with a disability, because they have often received a lower level of basic education, and because vocational training has to be adapted for them.

5. The application of new technologies which increase productivity may provide scope for reducing the working week and/or creating a more flexible organisation of both work time and workplace. Disabled people who find it hard to work for long, uninterrupted sessions may be given new opportunities, possibly the chance to work from home. House-bound disabled people would certainly benefit from it.

6. Technological innovations have undermined the security of formerly stable jobs within companies (the primary segment of the internal labour market). This mainly affects older employees, and consequently also many of the no longer fully-able employees.

The influence of these factors – which are sometimes enabling, sometimes limiting – is uneven for the entire disabled population. Some factors are, for instance, beneficial for the employment of physically or sensory disabled people but not for mentally disabled people. Furthermore, much depends on the way in which the technical innovations are introduced. But it is difficult to evaluate the actual influence on the demand-side in the labour market: 'Changes in work organisation, task contents or hierarchical structures – as a result or in conjunction with technological innovation – are after all of a qualitative nature, and no statistical tools are available to map out these processes of change in a representative way' (Berckmans, 1996: 391).

Another approach to studying developments in labour is to look at the international distribution of labour and influence thereof on various types of jobs. For this purpose, Reich divides work up in routine production services, in-person services and symbolic-analytic services (Reich, 1991).

Routine production services contain assembly line work as well as tasks performed by low and mid-level management in connection with repetitive checks on subordinates' work and the enforcement of standard operating procedures, and particular computer tasks e.g. the processing of financial transactions.

In-person services also contain routine services but in-person servers are in direct contact with the ultimate beneficiaries of their work.

Symbolic analysts solve, identify and broker problems by manipulating symbols. In other words, it is creative work.

In the industrialised countries, a number of routine production services come under heavy pressure from automation and delocation of production activities. In some client-based services, there is a lot of potential growth, but a pre-requisite would be government spending, and the latter is clearly being cut back. Services in the commercial sector are furthermore prone to being automated. However, most client-based services cannot be delocated. The only jobs which are increasing are those of the symbolic-analysts, but this type of work is not suitable for everyone, neither is it confined to national boundaries.

People with a disability can be found in one of three types of jobs, but, as noted earlier, they are increasingly disappearing from routine production services. In the non-commercial client-based services they are mostly clients and not service-providers, and in commercial services they only get a chance when the work does not require direct customer contact. Disabled people doing symbolic-analytical work are rare, even though it is mostly in that sector that examples of 'successful' disabled artists or scientists are given much publicity. Those disabled from when they were young are often poorly qualified, which means they are not eligible for symbolic-analytical work, and those who became disabled at a later stage would only be able to do this type of work if they used to do it before.

This representation of facts is probably only schematic, but it undermines the sometimes naive optimism expressed by some studies into the results of technological innovations for the job opportunities of people with disabilities. When one looks no further than the technological opportunities, optimism is justified, but when the developments are placed in a wider context, it soon turns into pessimism.

Will people with disabilities in the (near) future have to abandon the world of work for a life without work? This seems almost inevitable unless the boundary between both worlds is drawn less sharply. It has been demonstrated that the employment opportunities for people with a disability are often not only restricted by their disability but also by characteristics such as poor education, advanced age, or a combination of both. The segments of the labour market where low-educated and certainly (low-qualified) older employees can still fit in are also the segments where most people with disabilities have to find refuge. We should remind the reader at this stage that the sizeable group of (light to moderately) mentally disabled people and people with sensory or physical disabilities from an early age often hold few qualifications. Obtaining or returning to paid employment consequently poses the same problem for 'work disabled people', the unskilled long-term unemployed and the older unemployed. All these groups have become more dependent on benefits since the mid-Seventies. It has plunged the welfare state into a crisis, because the number of beneficiaries has become so large that the people making national insurance payments are unable or unwilling to support them any longer. Over the past twenty years, dozens of measures have been taken to help welfare recipients return to work. Their success rate was limited, since those who managed to find jobs were quickly replaced by newly redundant people or by unemployed youngsters.

This phenomenon is being called 'the new social issue', or 'the new exclusion'. At the heart of this issue is the relationship between work and non-work (Rosanvallon, 1995; Van Steenberge, 1995; Paugam, 1996). One of the solutions put forward is to use the benefits as payment, using a wider interpretation of work, to include activities which are useful to society but which are not rewarded in the traditional way. The consensus is gradually growing that 'working for benefits' should be allowed or even imposed on some groups, on condition that the work carried out is a useful training ground increasing the chances of real employment. The opportunity to earn extra on top of benefits is also being expanded. Furthermore, it is being investigated how unpaid activities, e.g. in the voluntary sector, could be given a higher social status, but the dominant work-ethos precludes this. The activities which should help benefit recipients return to work are mainly sited in a (partially) newly created sector called 'the social economy', of which customer-related services form an integral part (Europese Commissie, 1994).

These and other measures (for Belgium and the Netherlands, see Van Steenberge, 1995; for Germany, see Schmid, 1995) extend the labour market with provisions which are called 'transitional labour markets' because they are not intended to retain workers for the duration of their entire careers, but to bridge the gaps in the careers of an increasing number of people in a flexible way. The gaps could be transitional periods from full-time to part-time work, between work and education or vocational training, between work and being on the dole or on disability benefit, between domestic life and work, or between work and retirement.

Each 'bridge' could take on various forms. Schmid (1995: 447) sums up a few possibilities for the bridge between unemployment (possibly also incapacity to work) and work: 'The various forms of bridging mechanisms, both potential and those already in use, can be arranged in a continuum according to the degree of subsidy and proximity to the "regular labour market": temporary public jobs, the establishment of social enterprises, long-term wage subsidies for hiring the unemployed in the private sector, short-term recruitment subsidies for hard-to-place people, subsistence allowances (replacing unemployment benefits) for unemployed people starting their own business.' The number of jobs in bridging arrangements is increasing and disabled people can undoubtedly benefit from them.

The current job market is undergoing big changes of which we have mentioned but a few. The future is very uncertain, although a few possible scenarios present themselves (Boisonnat, 1995). In the light of what we know already, we will draw a few conclusions for the (re-)integration policy.

4 Implications for the (Re-)Integration Policy

In most European countries, (re-)integration measures for people with disabilities were first introduced in the Fifties and Sixties, when the labour market was very different from what it is now. A large part of the reserve work force consisted of partially able workers. The demand for workers was so great that functional and professional rehabilitation offered those people the prospect of a proper job. For those who dropped out, there was room in sheltered employment. The question is whether this reintegration system is still sufficient today.

4.1 How Specific Should the Policy Be?

The observation that people with disabilities are definitely not the only problem group in the job market, and furthermore that they often share characteristics with other problem groups, throws doubt on the benefit of a separate policy specifically for disabled people (Semlinger, 1989). In many countries, an entire system of legal provisions, employment agencies, training organisations, financial stimuli and 'reserved' jobs (whether or not in sheltered employment) has been established. From the late Seventies, when the unemployment crisis became an enduring problem, similar initiatives sprung up for other groups who were also excluded from the labour market. Employers were consequently approached by various training organisations trying to set up 'on the job training' for their client group, as well as by several specialised agencies each requesting special treatment for their target group, backed up by a wide array of start-up grants, efficiency subsidies, exemptions from social insurance contributions *et cetera*. A market of target groups has taken shape where the vendors try to market their 'goods' with the most attractive packaging, regularly hampering each other. The target groups bear distinct names, but in practice they greatly overlap each other. The categories work-disabled, long-term unemployed, unskilled, the poor, the underprivileged and women are, after all, not mutually exclusive. The extent of political attention for the individual target groups and the resulting amount of support are variable. New measures continuously abound to selectively benefit one group or the other.

Despite the above observations, policies for people with disabilities should not be abandoned. Some policy tools which do not exist for other target groups – e.g. functional rehabilitation and specific training courses (e.g. for people with serious sight or hearing disabilities) – would disappear along with them. Once the preparation period for starting or returning to work is over – and for some groups, like mentally disabled people, even during that period – it should be investigated how the measures aimed at the disabled people who still belong to at least one other target group could fit in with initiatives organised for that particular group. The way to achieve this depends on the particular policy tool. When new 'on the job' training courses are set up for unskilled youngsters, mentally disabled people should be allowed to participate. When employers are being paid higher wage subsidies for employing long-term unemployed, agencies in charge of the return to work of people with disabilities should ensure that long-term unemployed disabled people can also benefit from it. When local development projects are being set up in underprivileged neighbourhoods, an attempt should be made to involve disabled people in them.

This approach requires that the professionals in charge of integrating disabled people into the labour market would be less frequently based in separate organisations, but rather in organisations catering for other target groups. This method is comparable with introducing special needs teachers in main-stream education instead of isolating them in special schools. Custom-made policy should not disappear, just be less segregated.

4.2 (Re-)Integration Into Which Labour Market?

For most disabled people who have health problems combined with characteristics of other problem groups in the labour market, a direct introduction into the regular labour market has become extremely difficult. They mainly end up in so-called transitional labour markets, which the government can regulate to some extent through subsidised jobs. There are several ways of ensuring that people with disabilities are filling an appropriate number of these posts. One way is a general anti-discrimination ruling, like the 'Americans with Disabilities Act'. Another way is legislation to guarantee equal job opportunities, for instance the Canadian 'Employment Equity Act'. Those regulations should not necessarily be restricted to transitional labour markets, but in countries where as yet no legislation of that nature exists (e.g. Belgium) a limited introduction in these markets could be a first step.

Since the second half of the Eighties, the supply of part-time work has soared in Europe. This can be beneficial for disabled people who find it hard or impossible to cope with full-time work. Since it is mainly women who work part-time, disabled women – a very marginal group in the labour market – may get the best opportunities here. Often the social security system prohibits taking up a part-time job or even a low-paid full-time job. Of the three main invalidity benefits in Belgium, only the benefits to victims of job-related illnesses and work accidents do not restrict participation in the labour market, because they can be freely combined with an earned income. The illness and invalidity benefits can only be combined with a salary for a fixed period and to a particular level. Income support, the benefit designed to replace an income, is not supposed to be combined with any earned income at all.

Those people with disabilities entitled to benefits usually come under the last two categories. In the Belgian unemployment benefit system, it has recently become possible to earn a little extra on top of benefits through the 'Local Employment Agencies' (PWAs). A comparable measure for people on invalidity benefits should give a number of disabled people the opportunity to participate in the labour market and to top up their income. The introduction into transitional labour markets would also be much easier if the opportunities of combining an earned income with benefits were extended.

In a society where much unskilled labour is dwindling away because particular tasks disappear or because the training requirements for the same old jobs become more intricate, the group with mental disabilities poses a special problem. It is questionable whether they benefit much from the anti-discrimination legislation of the American type. The crucial question in this context is: when should a mentally disabled person be considered able to fulfil the 'essential requirements of the job' and which 'reasonable accommodations' could be expected from the employer? From comments on this issue (Bruyere, s.d), it appears that a huge amount of individual support is usually required. The 'supported-employment' initiatives which are gradually taking off even in Western Europe offer this kind of support. However, it often concerns involvement in unpaid work. Not necessarily because the employer is not prepared to pay, but because an earned income would automatically mean a reduction in benefit payments (see above). The expansion of support initiatives, combined with changes in the benefit system would give many mentally disabled people a real chance to work in the labour market.

In most European countries, people with mental disabilities constitute the largest group among the employees in sheltered workplaces. Recent changes in the labour market are casting a shadow over the future of these workplaces. Insofar as they depend on sub-contract work for factories, they are suffering from the knock-on effect of the general decline in industrial labour. Much 'simple' work is disappearing because it is being automated or moved away to countries with cheap labour. New markets, both in sub-contract work and for own products appear elusive or fail to cater for more than just a few jobs. More complex activities can only be accomplished when better-skilled personnel is recruited, and when investments are made in good quality machinery. The additional personnel is, by definition, not mentally disabled and in many cases not disabled in any other way. Until now, sheltered employment has been organised in a factory setting. There is little future for this model. The only opportunity for growth lies in the service sector, and that type of work cannot be brought to the workplace; the employees and support workers will have to step outside. Spatial integration becomes a necessity. Sheltered employment will start to lean closely to 'supported employment'. In several countries, workplaces (as organisations) have already stepped outside their own walls, but in others, the integrated model develops next to the segregated workplace, and they compete for government money.

4.3 New Policy Tools or a Different Approach?

After examining the various measures implemented by the German government to promote the employment of disabled people (compulsory employment, rehabilitation and training courses, grants to employers, adaptation of the workplace, etc.), Semlinger (1988 and 1989) came to the conclusion that the support services to employers especially have to be reinforced. It is the only way to ensure that employers do not avoid their obligations, and to create a positive attitude towards the support services. The current need is not so much for new measures, but for more advocates to promote the case with employers and to support them. They can adapt general measures for the specific requirements of a particular job, obtain the necessary social support from colleagues, make suggestions to adapt the job profile, give or organise training in the workplace, et cetera. This custom-made support service becomes even more important as job profiles and work charters become less standard, and careers become more varied.

References

Berckmans, P., De impact van technologische innovatie op de vraagzijde van de arbeidsmarkt, in: Steunpunt Werkgelegenheid, Arbeid en Vorming, De arbeidsmarkt in Vlaanderen, Katholieke Universiteit Leuven, 1996, p. 391-405.

Berthoud, R., The 'Medical' Assessment of Incapacity: a Case Study of Research and Policy, Journal of Social Security Law, 1995, (2), p. 61-85.

Boissonnat, J., Le travail dans vingt ans. Paris: Odile Jacob, 1995.

Brandt, F., Ursachen für die Schwierigkeiten bei der Eingliederung von Schwerbehinderten auf dem allgemeinen Arbeitsmarkt, Bundesministerium für Arbeit und Sozialordnung (Hrsg.), Forschungsbericht Sozialforschung 117, Bonn, 1985.

Bruyere, S.M. (s.d.), Working Effectively with Persons Who Have Cognitive Disabilities, in: S.M. Bruyere (Ed.), Implementing the ADA, School of Industrial and Labor Relations – Cornell University, Ithaca.

Christmann, H., Die arbeitsmarktpolitische Problematik der Vermittlung Schwerbehinderter und deren Integration in den Arbeitsmarkt, in: E. Knappe, B. Frick (Hrsg.), Schwerbehinderte und Arbeitswelt, Frankfurt/New York, Campus Verlag, 1988, p. 73-79.

Dench, S., *et al.*, The Recruitment and Retention of People With Disabilities, The Institute for Employment Studies, Brighton, 1996.

Europese commissie, Groei, concurrentievermogen, werkgelegenheid – Naar de 21e eeuw: wegen en uitdagingen – Witboek, Bureau voor officiële publikaties der Europese Gemeenschappen, Luxemburg, 1994.

Frick, B., Interne Arbeitsmärkte und betriebliche Schwerbehindertenbeschäftigung: theoretische Analysen und empirische Befunde, Campus Verlag, Frankfurt/New York, 1992.

Grammenos, S., Disabled Persons. Statistical Data, second edition, Office for Official Publications of the European Communities, Luxembourg, 1995.

Hibbeln, J.G., W. Velema, Het WAO debâcle. De fatale missers van wettenmakers en uitvoerders, Jan van Arkel, Utrecht, 1993.

Martin, J., *et al.*, OPCS Surveys of Disability in Great Britain, Report 4, Disabled Adults: Services, Transport and Employment, HMSO, London, 1989.

McNeil, J.M., *et al.*, Work Status, Earnings, and Rehabilitation of Persons With Disabilities, in: S. Thompson-Hoffman, I.F. Storck (Eds.), Disability in the United States; A Portrait From National Data, Springer, New York, 1991, p. 133-160.

Oliver, M., The Politics of Disablement, Macmillan, London, 1990.

Paugam, S. (Ed.), L'exclusion. L'état des savoirs, Editions La Découverte, Paris, 1996.

Prescott-Clarke, P., Employment and Handicap, Social and Community Planning Research, London, 1990.

Ravaud, J.-F., *et al.*, Le chômage des personnes handicapées. L'apport d'une explication en termes de discrimination à l'embauche, Archives maladies professionelles, 1995, 56, (6), p. 445-456.

Reich, R.B., The Work of Nations. Preparing Ourselves for 21st-Century Captalism, Alfred A. Knopf, New York, 1991.

Rendenbach, I., Ökonomie der Schwerbehindertenbeschäftigung. Eine marktorientierte Perspektive, Campus Verlag, Frankfurt/New York, 1990.

Rosanvallon, P., La nouvelle question sociale. Repenser l'Etat-Providence, Editions du Seuil, Paris, 1995.

Schmid, G., Is Full Employment Still Possible? Transitional Labour Markets as a New Strategy of Labour Market Policy, Economic and Industrial Democracy, 1995, 16, p. 429-456.

Semlinger, K., Staatliche Intervention durch Dienstleistungen. Funktionsweise und Steuerungspotential – untersucht am Beispiel der technischen Beratung zur Förderung der betrieblichen Integration Behinderter, Sigma, Berlin, 1988.

Semlinger, K., Zielgruppendifferenzierung und Politik-Marketing in der Rehablitation, in: D. Sadowski, I.M. Rendenbach (Hrsg.), Neue Zielgruppen in der Schwerbehindertenpolitik, Campus Verlag, Frankfurt/New York, 1989, p. 195-217.

Sly, F., *et al.*, Disability and the Labour Market: Findings from the Labour Force Survey, Labour Market Trends, 1995, December, p. 439-459.

Statistics Canada, Adults with Disabilities: Their Employment and Education Characteristics, 1991 Health and Activity Limitation Survey, Statistics Canada, 1993.

Stone, D.A., The Disabled State, Macmillan, Houndmills, 1984.

Van Steenberge, J., *et al.*, Niet-arbeid? Wel arbeid!, Koning Boudewijnstichting, Brussel, 1995.

Yelin, E.H., Disability and the Displaced Worker, Rutgers University Press, New Brunswick, 1992.

Factors related to the chances of labour market inclusion or exclusion for persons with a disability

Erik Samoy/ University of Leuven/ Department of Sociology / Sociology of Social Policy/Nov. 1996

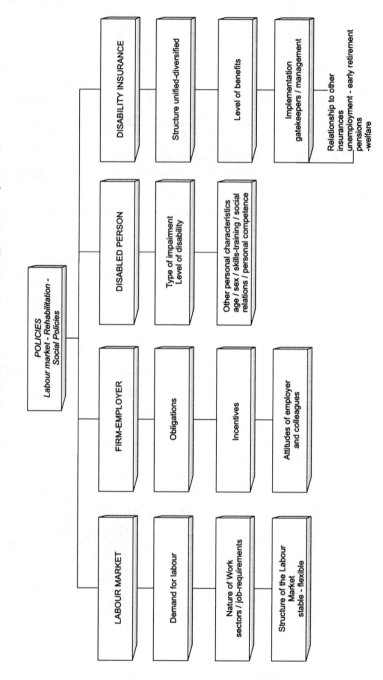

POLICIES
Labour market - Rehabilitation - Social Policies

LABOUR MARKET
- Demand for labour
- Nature of Work sectors / job-requirements
- Structure of the Labour Market stable - flexible

FIRM-EMPLOYER
- Obligations
- Incentives
- Attitudes of employer and colleagues

DISABLED PERSON
- Type of impairment Level of disability
- Other personal characteristics age / sex / skills-training / social relations / personal competence

DISABILITY INSURANCE
- Structure unified-diversified
- Level of benefits
- Implementation gatekeepers / management
  - Relationship to other insurances unemployment - early retirement pensions -welfare

Integration of Disabled People in the Workforce: Decisive Factors in the United Kingdom?

Patricia Thornton and *Neil Lunt*

1 An Introduction to UK Policy

Economic and ideological factors have framed recent governments' responses to disability employment issues in the United Kingdom. Economic policy has shifted markedly towards supply-side responses, with an emphasis on uninhibited market mechanisms as solutions to economic problems. Government has sought to stimulate competition and to encourage individual enterprise and incentive to work; regulation is thought to interfere with this process. Thus, government has intervened as little as possible in the economy and the labour market. Its aim has been to free up markets and eliminate controls. Deregulation has aimed to reduce the administrative burden faced by firms. An ideological aversion to 'big government' and a commitment to 'rolling back the frontiers of the state', as well as economic reasons, have justified non-intervention.

At the same time, a high profile disabled people's movement rejects patronage, challenging the traditional view that people deserve special provisions on grounds of disability. The Independent Living Movement has campaigned for individual rights to self-determination. The rhetoric of civil rights has helped to justify the retreat from policies of social obligation and the dismantling of practices which, in theory at least, protected the collective employment position of disabled people.

The increasing cost to the public exchequer of the growth in out-of-work disability benefits has been a prominent concern. The Department of Social Security (DSS) has promoted supply-side measures, both by reducing take-up of out-of-work benefits and by introducing a new in-work benefit for those on low earnings. Institutional divisions mean that responsibility for labour market policies rests with the Department for Education and Employment (DfEE), which has incorporated the long-standing Department of Employment. Despite the impression given by this recent amalgamation, the policies of DSS and the Employment division of DfEE have begun to show signs of convergence.

1.1 Current Strategy

For many years, the United Kingdom strategy to promote employment of disabled people has been encouragement and persuasion, not compulsion or regulation. This approach has had two strands. The first supposes that financial incentives can encourage disabled people to take up, or return to, work. A limited in-work, non-contributory social security benefit, practical help to access work, and priority access to training opportunities have been targeted at disabled people on the margins of work. At the same time, out-of-work contributory benefits have been restricted.

The second strand has comprised non-legislative measures to influence both employers' attitudes towards disabled workers and their recruitment and employment practices. This reliance on the 'voluntary' approach was aptly demonstrated by the Government's response to the European Commission's Green Paper on European Social Policy. That stated that the most effective way to promote job opportunities for people with disabilities is to get employers to recognise the abilities of disabled people and the business case for employing them (Employment Department, 1994, Annex 2).

The Disability Discrimination Act 1995 (DDA) – a measure which the Government implemented under pressure – underlined the reliance on individualistic solutions to structural problems. Government had successfully opposed comprehensive civil rights legislation, which it considered too sweeping and difficult to target on the groups who need most help. The costs to business and the assumed consequent effect on international competitiveness were fundamental concerns.

The UK now has no compulsory employment legislation. With the repeal of much of the ineffective, although symbolically important, Disabled Persons (Employment) Act 1944[1] there are no legislative duties on employers to ensure that disabled people are fairly represented in their workforce, no mechanisms for enforcing obligations and no penalties for breaking the law. Rather, under the DDA, employers of 20 or more workers have a duty to ensure that they do not discriminate against a disabled applicant or employee. Despite the new individual right not to be discriminated against, the disabled worker must prove his or her case and the wrongful employer need pay no penalties, other than any agreed compensation to the individual. There is no external body with powers of investigation into employers' practices and no Equal Opportunities Commission, comparable to those set up in the UK to protect against discrimination on grounds of race or gender.

The abandonment of compulsory employment legislation is not as abrupt as it might at first appear. The 1944 Act, in particular its provisions for compulsory employment, was subject to repeated reviews. From 1973, the intention of governments and their agencies was to abolish the quota, universally recognised as unworkable. Campaigners, however, argued for its retention, in a strengthened form, until an acceptable alternative became credible. Governments preferred to pursue policies of persuasion and education: employers were to change their attitudes, adopt good practice and willingly take on disabled employees, without legislative 'sticks'. Enforcement of the law would be an unwarranted intervention in the labour market, not in accord with overall labour market policies. For many years, there was a policy vacuum, with no sanctions imposed on employers who evaded the quota obligation and no alternative right to employment for disabled workers.

UK employers have never been obliged by law to maximise the employment of disabled people through creating barrier-free work environments and production processes. The DDA provisions include a duty to take 'steps as it is reasonable' to alter the working conditions or working environment to facilitate the employment of an identified disabled person. The Act does not provide for funds for employers to remove disabling barriers. Any such action must be paid for from an individual disabled employee's allocation for Access to Work (a fund administered by Employment Services); an employer contribution to the cost was introduced in 1996. There have been almost no direct financial incentives to employers of disabled workers in open employment. There is no minimum wage, and employers can expect low-waged employees to supplement their incomes through in-work means-tested social security benefits, first introduced for families with children, and now available for disabled workers.[2] However, wage subsidies apply in supported placement schemes, a growing method of placing less productive workers in open employment, in part as a less costly alternative to sheltered workshops.[3] Supported placements tend to target people with learning disabilities, while in sheltered workshops physically disabled employees have predominated. The overall sheltered employment sector remains small, compared with that in other countries participating in the expert meeting.

1.2 Withdrawal of the State

With the abolition of compulsory employment legislation and the introduction of an anti-discrimination law which depends on aggrieved individuals taking action, central Government's policy role withdrew to one of advisor and enabler. More and more, employers have been encouraged to improve voluntarily their recruitment and employment practices. Government has placed faith in local employers' networks, as vehicles for affecting such changes. Trades union involvement is not well developed, especially at the local level, and has received little encouragement from Government.

There are no formal arrangements for the representation of disabled people at the workplace.

The delivery of services is devolved to governmental agencies at the local level. Placement Assessment and Counselling Teams (PACTs) offer specialist services to disabled people who need help outside mainstream programmes; they also work with prospective employers. Rehabilitation is now meant to be provided by non-governmental agencies under contract to the PACTs. Mainstream training is delivered through local Training and Enterprise Councils (TECs) giving priority to disabled people. TECs operate under output-related contracts which can make it more difficult for them to serve disabled clients who need potentially unprofitable levels of support.

2 Structure of the Paper

Confining our discussion to the title of the book – rehabilitation of partially disabled workers – is not straightforward.

Rehabilitation – in the sense of intervention to ensure that workers who become (more) disabled retain their jobs or return to other suitable work, whether with the same employer or elsewhere – has rarely featured in UK policy and practice. Employment Department 'resettlement' or 'advisory' services, which attracted criticism for lengthy delays in arranging placements, have seldom practised early intervention at the workplace. The old rehabilitation centres tended to serve longer-term unemployed disabled people. The policy response to criticism of the ineffectiveness of such centres was to close them, and to promote special schemes to tackle barriers to employment. Thus, there has historically been little investment in strategies to adapt the individual to job opportunities.

Workplace rehabilitation has never been a feature of UK provision. There are no obligations on employers to ensure the retention of employees who become disabled, and the notion of disability management at the workplace is only now gaining some limited currency, mainly through the activities of voluntary sector service-providers. In general, UK policy has not distinguished between return to work of those who have left employment because of disability and entry to work of disabled people who have never worked. Only recently, in response to the concerns over the growth of contributory incapacity benefits, a distinction has begun to emerge, although not clearly articulated.

Equally problematic, for this chapter, is the very limited recognition in the UK of the concept of a 'partially disabled' worker. The UK incapacity benefits system is characterised as 'sick-or-fit' or 'all-or-nothing'. Employment opportunities for incapacity benefit recipients are limited to therapeutic work, approved by a medical practitioner, with hours and earnings limits. Partial capacity in work is provided for only through the new means-tested benefit, Disability Working Allowance, restricted to those on low earnings.

The question we have been asked to address is whether increasing individual responsibilities of employers and employees is a better method, than coercion of employers, to increase participation of partially disabled workers in the workforce. We have chosen to pursue this question by examining three elements of current UK policy:
- social security policies which aim to reduce dependence on out-of-work benefits and introduce financial incentives to (re)enter work;
- inducements to employers to review and change their practices voluntarily;
- the new right, introduced by the DDA, against discrimination in employment.
In considering the first two aspects, we draw on UK research. Discussion of the third element unavoidably must remain theoretical, given implementation of the employment provisions of the law only occurred in December 1996. First, we take a brief look at how disability is defined in the UK, and review the situation of disabled people in the labour force.

3 Definitions of Disability

The DDA introduced a new definition of disability. That definition relates to the new right not to be discriminated against in employment, in getting goods and services, and in buying or renting land or property.

The Act defines disability as 'a physical or mental impairment which has a substantial or long-term adverse effect on a person's ability to carry out normal day-to-day activities'. Government guidance defines the terms 'impairment', 'substantial', 'long-term' and 'normal day-to-day activities'. It is important to note that normal activities are functionally defined, in terms of mobility, dexterity, hearing, memory and so on. Also covered by the Act are the following: those who have had a disability in the past; people with severe disfigurements which have no effect on their ability to carry out normal activities; and people with progressive conditions, such as cancer or HIV infection, where impairments are likely to become substantial. Unlike the 1944 Act which it replaced, the DDA does not define 'disability' in relation to its effect on a person's ability to obtain or retain paid work. Voluntary registration as a disabled person for the purpose of employment, which was in any case under-subscribed, was abolished.

For benefits within the social security system, functional measures such as 'requiring attention or supervision from another person', 'unable or virtually unable to walk', 'degree of disablement', are fundamental to the system. For those particular sickness and disability benefits which are dependent on being 'incapable of work', this must be 'by reason of some specific disease or bodily or mental disablement'. There is no labour market criterion.

Despite disability movement campaigns, notably by the British Council of Disabled People (BCODP), the 'social model' of disability is not recognised by official definitions of disability. BCODP believes that disability should be characterised as 'the loss or limitation of opportunities to take part in the mainstream of life in the community on an equal level with others due to physical or social barriers'.

4 Disabled People in the Labour Force

Estimates of employment and unemployment among disabled people vary. Differences in survey results can be attributed to a number of factors: definitions used, the overall purposes of surveys, methods of questioning, sources, the populations covered, and the times when surveys were conducted. In 1997 the results are expected of a new 'baseline' survey of disabled people's participation in the labour force, using the definition of disability in the DDA.

The Labour Force Survey of winter 1994/95 found that 11 per cent of the working age population in private households in Great Britain (3.8 million) has a work-limiting long-term health problem or disability – 2.1 million men and 1.6 million women. The economic activity rate for disabled people of working age was less than half that of non-disabled people (40 per cent compared with 83 per cent). The employment rate was 32 per cent compared with 76 for non-disabled people. Unemployment rates among disabled people were around two-and-a half times those for non-disabled people (21.6 per cent compared with 9.0 per cent). (For a detailed analysis of the Labour Force Survey see Sly *et al.* 1995.) An earlier Government commissioned survey (Prescott-Clarke, 1990) found that 22 per cent of 'occupationally handicapped' but economically active men and women 'wanted work'. These rates were almost twice as high as those for economically active men and women in the general population.

5 Disability Benefit Policies

Public expenditure on benefits for sick or disabled people accounts for almost one quarter of the total spent on social security benefits. The number of people receiving the contributory, out-of-work Invalidity Benefit (IVB), now superseded by the Incapacity Benefit (IB), tripled between 1975 and 1995. Reasons for the increase are contested but the most definitive analysis saw as the main cause recipients staying on the benefit for longer, rather than moving back into work (Lonsdale *et al.*, 1993). The policy response was two-fold: to tighten eligibility criteria for the benefit and reduce its level; and to introduce a new in-work benefit, designed as an incentive to move from Invalidity (now Incapacity) Benefit (and other minor benefits) into work.

5.1 Incapacity Benefit

There were important changes to the disability benefits system in April 1995. IVB, the main benefit payable to chronically sick and disabled people after 28 weeks, and the shorter-term Sickness Benefit, were replaced by a new incapacity benefit (IB). This change was accompanied by the introduction of a new system for assessing capacity to work, including the 'all work' test. The rationale of the reforms was to stem the rising number of IVB recipients. Numbers drawing the benefit grew from 600,000 in 1978-9 to 1.5 million in 1993-4. Expenditure had doubled in real term since 1982-3 and was forecast to increase a further 50 per cent by 1999. Growth in expenditure was attributed to weak controls on access to and continued receipt of the benefit, considered by Government to be ill-focused and subject to abuse. The reforms sought to re-focus provision on people who were 'genuinely' incapable of work through sickness or disability, by tightening eligibility criteria and reducing the level of benefit.

Eligibility tests for income replacement disability benefits are now based initially on self-assessment of functional capacity. The 'own occupation' test assesses the ability of individuals to do their own usual work, supported by a medical certificate issued by their doctor, and applies for the first 28 weeks of a claim. After 28 weeks, the 'all work' test assesses capacity to do any work. (Those with no usual occupation are subject to the all work test immediately.) This test limits consideration to the degree of 'functional ability' to carry out activities.[4] Limits on ability are scored; a total of 15 points qualifies. Claimants complete a questionnaire and statements are supplied by medical practitioners and specialists. Claimants may be asked to undergo a medical examination if required by the decision-makers (the Benefit Agency Medical Service). The IB 'all work test' thus contains no reference to labour market conditions. Under IVB, incapacity for work had been judged by reference to medical condition in the context of factors such as age, skills and experience.

Government projections were that an additional 250,000 individuals would be available for work as a result of the changes. This estimate included 190,000 previous recipients of IVB, and 55,000 new claimants of IB, with potential savings of £1,720 million by 1997-8. Savings would also be assisted by the reduced rates IB would be payable at, as a result of abolishing earnings related-additions, changes to dependency and age allowances, and increasing the qualifying period for long-term benefit levels.

Figures for the first six months show that 47,310 individuals were disallowed benefits and moved on to unemployment benefit and social assistance. From October 1996 the main route for ineligible IB claimants is on to the new Jobseekers Allowance. There will be a time-lag before the number of previous IVB recipients, who were given transitional arrangements, are re-assessed under the new 'all work' regime.

Although the changes are in an early stage, some problems have been identified, by welfare rights commentators and practitioners, about how procedures may affect certain groups. For example, there has been concern that those with fluctuating conditions may not have their circumstances adequately captured on the day of assessment. There is some evidence that people with mental health needs can be disadvantaged by the different procedures designed for them. More generally, critics of the changes have argued that IVB was in fact a well-targeted benefit; its recipients had serious and long-term health difficulties and were in need of its provision. Moreover, recipients tended to be ex-manual workers and less likely to have occupational pensions and permanent health insurance, a group particularly affected by the reduced rates of payment.

5.2 Disability Working Allowance

An innovation in disability policy was the introduction of Disability Working Allowance (DWA) in April 1992. This social security benefit is intended to encourage disabled people off benefits and into work, by topping up low earnings. Its introduction reflects the employment policy assumption that improving incentives will encourage those at the margin to engage in increased economic activity.

Prior to the introduction of DWA, the social security system created disincentives for disabled people to enter work in two ways. First, there was little possibility of building on partial capacity for work within the benefits system. IB recipients can undertake paid work of up to 16 hours a week (earning no more than £44) only if of benefit to their health; an estimated two per cent of recipients use this option. Secondly, disabled people were unable to experiment and test their capacity for work without losing entitlement to long-term benefits. The IB rules mean that return to the benefit at the same rate is permissible only within eight weeks of taking up a job. DWA has much more favourable 'linking rules': if the job does not work out and the person has to resign, return to their former rate of IB is safeguarded for up to two years, as long as the person is still incapable of work.

DWA is a tax-free, non-contributory benefit. It is means-tested and the amount payable depends on the total income of the claimant's family. DWA is paid on top of low wages or self-employed earnings for people whose disability puts them at a 'disadvantage in getting a job'. People must be working for 16 hours or more and must have received IB, one of the other two income replacement disability benefits[5] (or certain other premiums) *or* be receiving Disability Living Allowance (a non-means-tested 'costs of disability' benefit).

It was estimated that 50,000 people would successfully claim DWA. Compared with Government expectations, the results to date have been disappointing. At July 1996, the case-load was around 10,500. The number and proportion of new claimants responding to the incentive effect is increasing slowly, however. It had been assumed that 70 per cent of the estimated 50,000 claimants would be people who had taken jobs in response to the benefit; the rest were expected to be already in work. A Government-commissioned three-year study (Rowlingson and Berthoud, 1994; 1996) found that in October 1993, 18 months after introduction, only 200 of the 3,500 DWA claimants had been encouraged into work by the benefit.

DWA's effect on enabling people to move off incapacity benefits was initially negligible. In the period from spring 1992 to autumn 1995, only two per cent of the 1.5 million working-age recipients of one of the three main incapacity benefits moved off these benefits and into full-time work, almost all without the help of DWA (Rowlingson and Berthoud, 1996).

A secondary aim of DWA has been to act as a long-term subsidy for those in low-paid employment. In this respect, the benefit has exceeded expectations, as most recipients were already in work when they heard of it. It is not possible to tell from the published DWA statistics how far it has enabled recipients to progress in employment and move off benefit. The evaluation found that only a very small proportion of the study cohort had done so.

Some commentators suggest that structural aspects of DWA, such as the means-test and potential poverty trap, limit its use. There is some evidence that the way the benefit is promoted has limited take-up; awareness has been very low. Moreover, according to Rowlingson and Berthoud (1996) there is an in-built contradiction in the system. IB is conceived of as an *incapacity* benefit, that is for people whose *inability* to work is demonstrated. Yet, having received IB is a qualifying condition for DWA. Other commentators have argued that adjustments to benefits will have little effect. Being stereotyped as unemployed or as disabled may be greater barriers to work than any 'benefits trap'. The assumptions underlying DWA are firmly located in supply-side solutions and a belief in individual responsibility. There is a clear view in this policy of economic, rational actors acting at the margin to take-up opportunities that were previously not worthwhile. However, those job opportunities do not necessarily exist.

5.3 Alternative Approaches to Partial Capacity Provision

Disability campaign groups have for many years argued a case for a benefit which takes account of partial incapacity for work and which can be claimed both in and out of work. They have claimed that experience in other European countries may be transferable to the UK. Research commissioned from the Social Policy Research Unit by the Social Security Advisory Committee is examining alternative approaches to partial incapacity provision in six other countries (Thornton, Sainsbury and Barnes, forthcoming 1997).

6 Persuasion Policies

In this section, we examine what in the UK is known as the 'voluntary approach' to changing employers' practices, founded on persuasion not regulation. As we will show, the UK has used few financial rewards to pursue policies of persuasion. Rather, its principal strategy is to promote employer commitment to 'a positive approach' to employing disabled people.

6.1 Subsidies and Grants

UK Governments have tended to avoid financial rewards to employers as mechanisms for regulating the labour market in general. The recent announcement of a national insurance 'holiday', encouraging employers to take on anyone unemployed for two or more years, is novel in the UK context.

The idea that employers might be rewarded for taking on disabled workers is antithetical to the principles of the 1944 Act, which expected disabled people to be employed on merit and in equal competition. The few schemes that have been tried have not been promoted as 'financial incentives' to take on disabled workers. Rather, they are said to offer an opportunity to discover disabled people's skills and potential, and to deal with any practical concerns, so building on the 'business case' for employing disabled people. Currently, only one small scheme provides direct financial assistance to an employer. Under the Job Introduction Scheme, introduced in 1977, an employer in the private sector who takes on a disabled worker is paid a grant towards wages of £45 a week for a trial period of six weeks. The job must be expected to last for at least six months after the trial period has ended. When the grant stood at £40 per week, the scheme was reported in 1981 to be very successful, though the latest available figures suggest that numbers have dropped significantly.

In the past, financial support for employers was designed in the main to contribute towards the costs of adapting the working environment to meet the needs of a specified employee. However, take-up was always poor, and the few schemes tried have been abandoned. Schemes once targeted at the employer, such as the Adaptions to Premises and Equipment Scheme, have now been incorporated in the overall Access to Work (ATW) programme designed around the disabled employee. This programme, introduced in 1994 and administered by the Employment Service, can pay for physical alterations to the workplace, special equipment or adaptations to existing equipment, deaf awareness training for co-workers, job coaches to help familiarity with new tasks, adaptations of a vehicle or help with transport to work costs, a communicator at interview, and other practical needs. ATW will pay for 100 per cent of approved costs for unemployed disabled people or those changing employer, and 100 per cent of travel to work and communicator at interview costs, regardless of status. When first introduced, there were no costs to the employer. From April 1996, for those in work employers pay the first £300 each year and, thereafter, ATW will meet up to 80 per cent of the costs. All the costs in excess of £1,000 over three years will be met.

One of the aims of ATW is to increase the number of disabled people in the labour market by encouraging employers to recruit disabled people. The original stated aim was that half of the new entrants to ATW should be unemployed. However, a survey commissioned by the Employment Service and conducted one year after the start of ATW found that 92 per cent of the survey sample were already in paid work when they applied for ATW support (Beinart *et al.*, 1996).

Compensation for reduced productivity is found only within the special context of the Supported Employment Scheme. There has never been support for wage subsidies. In 1956, a review of the 1944 Act (the Piercy Report) rejected their implication that disabled people were less capable and a potential form of cheap labour. Disabled people's organisations see wage subsidies as demeaning. However, the extension of 'sheltered' work into open employment, for people who had been categorised as severely disabled and not capable of competitive work, has led to the introduction of a mechanism for subsidy. While employers are not compensated directly for reduced productivity, under the Supported Placements Scheme the employer pays only a portion of the wage and the state, through an agency, pays the remainder.

Research indicates reducing levels of employer awareness of programmes similar to those outlined above. In 1987, a government commissioned survey (Morrell, 1990) interviewed mainly personnel officers of establishments with 20 or more employees. It found awareness levels of over 50 per cent in relation to merely three special schemes, and only among employers with contact with the Disability Advisory Service. In the same study, 20 per cent had used the Job Introduction Scheme. A recent study of employers' practices (Dench et al., 1996) found that only 23 per cent of a random sample were aware of Access to Work and its predecessor special schemes; and only four per cent claimed some sort of contact with those provisions. These, and earlier, studies have found a not surprising association between contact with employment services for disabled people (such as the present day PACTs) and awareness of government schemes. The limited coverage by specialist employment services of potential employers, and particularly of small and medium-sized enterprises (SMEs), has been recurrently criticised.

6.2 Promoting Good Employment Practices

In the UK there are three strands to the promotion of good employment practices: encouragement to adopt voluntary 'codes' of practice, disability symbols, encouragement to join employer networks. A fourth measure, the regulatory obligation on large companies to publish a statement of policy in their annual report, by contrast, is seldom mentioned in governmental promotional material. Government expects employers to review their practices because, according to the rhetoric, it 'makes good business sense' to employ disabled people.

6.2.1 Good Practice Guides and Codes

Over the past 20 years, central government and its agencies have tried to influence employers' attitudes and practices with promotional material. In 1977, a 'Positive Policies' campaign was launched 'to develop enlightened internal company policies' and 55,000 firms were targeted with booklets outlining six main guidelines on recruitment, retention, training and career development, and modification and adaptation of equipment and premises. The government agency of the time (the Manpower Services Commission) found the campaign to have had 'minimal impact'; only one in five employers in a follow-up survey remembered having received and read the literature.

A non-statutory Code of Good Practice on the employment of disabled people was introduced in 1984, and updated in 1990 and in 1993. The document aimed to help companies specify their objectives and draw up a policy, rather than to set out targets or measures of achievement. Although 120,000 copies were distributed, Government commissioned research estimated that it was received by less than one-fifth of all employers (Morrell, 1990).

The DDA provided for a statutory Code of Practice. This 68 page, priced publication gives guidance to employers in interpreting the provisions of the Act relating to employment which came into effect on 2 December 1996.

6.2.2 Disability Symbols

Symbols marking good practice have a similarly long history. In 1979, a 'Fit for Work' campaign attempted to bolster the limited impact of Positive Policies, by conferring 100 awards each year to firms that made 'outstanding achievements in the employment of disabled people', measured by adherence to the same six guidelines. Award winners received a presentation plaque, citation and desk ornament and could use the award's emblem. The scheme lasted for 11 years but is reported to have had little impact.

The Disability Symbol, introduced in 1990, may be used on job advertisements and on recruitment literature. It is not awarded, but is adopted voluntarily by those employers who, after discussion with Employment Service officials, demonstrate an organisational commitment to good employment opportunities for disabled people, and are thus 'positive about disabled people'. Use of the symbol highlights five commitments: guaranteed job interviews to disabled applicants who meet the minimum criteria for a vacancy, consultation with a disabled employee at least once a year about his or her requirements at work, making every effort to keep a worker in employment if he or she becomes disabled, improving disability awareness among key employees, checking progress, planning ahead and informing all employees of progress and plans. The number of symbol users has increased from around 300 in June 1993 to over 2000 private and public sector companies in 1996.

The commissioning of a succession of surveys demonstrates the extent of the Government's investment in its lead strategy of increasing employer commitment to a positive approach to employing disabled people. The most recent survey (Dench et al., 1996) found that symbol users were more likely to have a written policy specifically addressing the employment of disabled people and more likely to try actively to attract applications from disabled people. However, symbol users were no more likely than non users to have disabled people in their workforce. Moreover, there is no clear evidence that symbol use led to improved practices. Over 40 per cent of symbol users in the survey reported that it had not made any difference to their practices. It seemed likely that registration as a symbol user attracted those employers who already had good practices in place.

6.2.3 Employer Networks

Although not promoted as official policy, peer group activities, such as the national Employers Forum on Disability and the small number of local employer networks, have been welcomed and encouraged by Government. The Employers Forum on Disability, financed entirely from subscriptions, has about 180 members, all large firms including many multi-national companies. An independent body, it is thought highly of by Government, and favourable references to it have appeared prominently in policy documents. The Government-commissioned survey of employers, already cited, found low levels of awareness and use of the Employers Forum and local employer networks. The small memberships of the latter have tended to be dominated by the larger, good practice employers, often local branches of members of the Employers Forum (Maginn and Meager, 1995).

Employer networks, and other means of branding 'good employers', are intended to set an example to less progressive firms. They may also be valuable as a source of information on employment services such as Access to Work, about which employers in the recent survey were notably ignorant. Dench *et al.* (1996) suggest that such networks might most usefully engage in proactive recruitment, given the prime difficulty employers reportedly face of achieving disabled applicants. However, this is not seen by networks as a main aim (Maginn and Meager, 1995).

6.2.4 Companies Act

In 1980, a regulatory measure joined the voluntary initiatives. The Companies (Director's Report) (Employment of Disabled People) Regulations 1980 were later incorporated in the Companies Act 1985. It placed a duty on all UK registered companies employing more than 250 people to include in their annual Directors' Report a statement of the policy applied during the previous year on recruitment, retention, training, promotion and career development of disabled people. Although the Act does not apply to public sector employers, both the Employment Department and the Department of Trade and Industry (who administer the Act) have advised that public sector employers should also adhere to its regulations. However, the requirement of the Companies Act is rarely highlighted by Government and there is no evidence about adherence or, indeed, whether policy statements bear any relation to practice.

6.2.5 Good Business Sense

An overt UK Government argument has been that business will gain, not lose, from having disabled people among its employees – that it 'makes good business sense'. The rhetoric is the culmination of a long campaign to convince the employer that the disabled worker is as good as someone who is not disabled. The dominant line of persuasion is that disabled workers should be valued not only for 'ability not disability', but also because they are potentially a more profitable asset to an employer than a non-disabled person. Employment Services literature stresses that in excluding disabled people 'you could be missing the best person for the job', and in retaining a disabled person 'you keep their skills and experience and you save the cost (and inconvenience) of replacing them'. Disabled people's organisations are equally keen to dispel the myth that disabled people are less productive and have bad sickness records.

Commentators elsewhere have pointed to the business advantages of being seen to employ disabled people, particularly in the service industry sector. Anecdotal evidence from France and from Canada suggests that being known to employ disabled people helps promote a fashionable image for a firm, and thus boost sales, trade or other business (Leichsenring and Strümpel, 1995).

The 'business sense' case is argued in terms of benefits which are likely to accrue, not disbenefits which will befall a firm which fails to comply. The North American concept of 'contract compliance', where a firm loses business if it does not demonstrate good employment practices, was unacceptable to UK governments set on non-interference in the market.

6.2.6 Discussion

There is little evidence that persuasion policies have had an impact on the level of recruitment of disabled people. Research consistently reports that employer prejudice is a major disincentive to work; while employers consistently state that the main reason for not employing disabled people is that none apply. We do not know whether 'good practice' strategies affect the job-seeking behaviour of disabled people. Policies aimed at 'setting an example', and those that seek to work through organisations in a voluntary way, have a long-term agenda. However, promotion of good employment practices has been part of government policy for nearly two decades, with no apparent affect on the quantity or quality of disabled people's employment.

Strategies to improve recruitment practices assume that vacancies are advertised and competitive interviews are held. Yet many employers, SMEs in particular, recruit by word-of-mouth. Studies have shown that the main way of finding a job is through hearing about it from someone who works there. Raising disability awareness among potential co-workers may be a more useful means of attracting disabled applicants. Strategies which focus on improving recruitment practices may be hampered by a mismatch between vacancies and the qualifications of disabled job-seekers. The Employment and Handicap survey carried out for the Employment Department in 1989 (Prescott-Clarke, 1990) found that 59 per cent of those who wanted work, in the economically active category, and 53 per cent of those in the category anticipating working in the next 12 months had no educational qualifications. The benefit trap also affects opportunities for training: recipients of IB have been excluded from training schemes aimed at the unemployed. The value of training allowances has in any case eroded. Moreover, jobs which do not require qualifications typically offer very low rates of pay which cannot meet the financial needs of many disabled people.

7 Anti-Discrimination Legislation

What will be the impact on employment practices of the new Disability Discrimination Act? As well as conferring on individual disabled people a right not to be discriminated against, the Act imposes a new obligation on employers of twenty or more staff to make adjustments for a disabled person, where it is reasonable to do so. Those rights and duties relate to recruitment, transfer, training, career progression and general treatment at work. The duty to make adjustments relates to physical features of the premises as well as to recruitment and employment practices.

Where there are complaints against employers of alleged unjustified discrimination, the conciliation service of the Advisory, Conciliation and Arbitration Service (ACAS) is available, and in the last resort there should be a remedy through an industrial tribunal. The individual may then obtain compensation and action against the cause of the grievance. However, the employer when responding to an individual's complaint has little responsibility to make the working environment less discriminatory. Rather, the employer settles terms with the individual.

It seems unlikely that adjustments arising from a single individual's needs will have a wider influence on work and workplace. Accommodation made for one person may be particular to his or her impairment and may not help the employment position of other disabled people. There are two dangers here: that issues become privatised between the individual and the firm, and that work and workplaces still contribute to social constructions of disability. Anti-discrimination legislation which operates according to known limitations of specific individuals can be contrasted with the approach of legally requiring employers to arrange work and workplace to maximise the employment of disabled people.

On the other hand, the experience of taking on and making accommodation for a disabled worker may lead to improved employment prospects for others with similar impairments. Research has consistently shown that those employers with experience of employing a disabled person are more favourably disposed towards taking on more.

However, the system may lead to the exclusion of disabled individuals less able to advocate for themselves. One of the main problems anticipated in the USA for the Americans with Disabilities Act 1990 (ADA) was how to make people suitably aware of their rights and the operation of the scheme. Clearly, an individual must have adequate education, training and support services to get to the position of being able to use the legal challenges. Advocacy and support may need to be offered for individual cases. In the UK, the onus falls on individuals to pursue their own grievances. Alternative civil rights legislation advanced in the failed Civil Rights (Disabled Persons) Bill 1994 saw an important role for a new Disability Rights Commission to monitor the act and investigate complaints independently. One key role of a Commission under this alternative legislative model would be to 'carry out general investigations with a view to determining whether the provisions of this Act are being complied with'.

The bid for a strengthened advocacy role would seem more closely modelled on other countries' experience of civil rights legislation.[6] Australia's Disability Discrimination Act (1992) is administered by the Human Rights and Equal Opportunity Commission under the direction of a Disability Discrimination Commissioner. The Commission can investigate complaints on its own or those brought to its attention. The Canadian Human Rights Commission enforces the Canadian Human Rights Act of 1977, to which disability was added in 1985. The Commission operates at arm's length from government; it deals with individual complaints of discrimination and promotes awareness of principles underlying human rights legislation. The Commission acts on behalf of aggrieved persons or initiates complaints on its own behalf.

The UK approach is relatively weak with regard to sanctions, with its emphasis upon conciliation. While Australia and the USA both prefer conciliation, there is the option of formal hearings and ultimately law suits. In Canada, after the Commission has investigated, a Human Rights tribunal can be appointed to take things further, ultimately levying a fine of $50,000 against firms.

Moreover, the UK law applies only to employers of 20 or more workers, representing only 65 per cent of the employed population, or four per cent of all firms. Justification is drawn from the USA, where the ADA covers employers with over 15 employees, but Australian discrimination legislation and Canadian human rights legislation do not exempt firms with lower numbers of employees.

In the UK, anti-discrimination legislation is relatively isolated, with few supportive measures. Other countries have accompanied anti-discrimination legislation with other measures and legislation. In Australia, when the Discrimination Act was introduced, a Disability Reform Package was also established with a range of training packages and schemes to assist to find work. There anti-discrimination legislation does not stand alone, but is supplemented by a range of equal opportunity legislation governed by states and government departments, and backed by further Federal provisions for encouraging employment opportunities and by fiscal packages.

Similarly, in the USA the 1973 Rehabilitation Act had outlined rights of disabled people in the federal workforce, enforced by the Equal Employment Opportunity Commission. Federal agencies were themselves expected to produce affirmative action plans and operate as model employers. Federal contractors, under contracts in excess of $2,500, had to produce affirmative action plans and make 'reasonable accommodation'. Recipients of federal financial assessment had similar obligations under the Act. Furthermore, at state level there are equal opportunity provisions, as well as additional human rights legislation. Turning to Canada, in 1991 the Canadian Governmental Strategy for Persons with Disabilities was introduced with a commitment of $158 million over 5 years. As in Australia, there is also a range of employment equity and equal opportunity measures – Employment Equity in the Public Service, Employment Equity Act and the Federal Contractors Programme, all introduced in 1986. The Employment Equity Act, under which disabled people are one of the four target groups, means more than treating persons in the same way; it also requires special measures and the accommodation of differences. Its aim is to identify and eliminate barriers and encourage positive policies and practices. Some Canadian provinces have attempted to shift this principle into the private sector.

Finally, although all countries have a range of financial measures and incentives to encourage employment of disabled workers, there may be an argument for strengthening these measures when introducing anti-discrimination legislation. In the USA for example, the Revenue Conciliation Act 1990 added an 'access credit' to the code which allows small businesses to claim against taxes for certain costs of ADA compliance. The aim of this legislation is especially to encourage small businesses. In the UK, the failed Civil Rights (Disabled Persons) Bill recognised that accommodations may unduly prejudice business operations. In addition to the nature and cost of changes, and the overall financial resources of workplaces and employers, another factor it considered was the availability of grants from public funds to defray the expense of any accommodation. Such considerations were absent from the Government proposals. The issue of where to situate costs of accommodation for anti-discrimination legislation bears on the nature of the obligation imposed and the ultimate success of policy.

8 Outlook for the UK?

We question what UK anti-discrimination legislation can achieve standing alone. Anti-discrimination laws have the advantage over the old quota scheme in that they may tackle the problem of underemployment, through confronting the kind of discrimination which prevents advancement at work. But a disabled person must be in employment or competing for a particular post before he or she can be protected; that is, able to perform the 'essential requirements' of the job. The Act does not extend to education and training. What is more, unless the nature of the job is changed before the onset of recruitment, the potential for disabled applicants remains constrained. There are particular doubts about whether the Act can improve the position of people with learning difficulties, who may require positions specially tailored to their abilities.

The effects of legislation against discrimination are notoriously difficult to measure. Does a low level of complaints against employers mean the law is working well, or badly? And how can employment practices be monitored and evaluated? These difficulties will be particularly pronounced in the UK where grievances are in the first instance a private concern, where employers have no obligations to report their practices, and where there are no powers of investigation.

That said, anti-discrimination legislation may have purposes other than just defending the rights of individuals in particular cases. It may have an important educative role; in Australia, for instance, legislation to eliminate discrimination also aimed to promote recognition and acceptance of the principle that disabled people have the same fundamental rights as the rest of the community. There may also be an important symbolic role for legislation. In Canada, for example, it is said that public debate surrounding employment equity and human rights has served to heighten the awareness of many employers as to their responsibilities. Will the new law in the UK achieve such educative and symbolic importance?

9 Concluding Discussion

In our introduction we noted the shift in the UK away from policies with a collective aim of promoting employment for disabled people as a group. Now, UK disability policy is weighted heavily in favour of individually-based solutions to employment. The state has withdrawn its responsibility to ensure that all sectors of society have a right to work, in favour of promoting opportunities for individual competition. The personal right not to be discriminated against is supported by individual systems of redress. The system of financial and practical support is targeted at the disabled individual. The disabled jobseeker competes in the market place, aided by training and in-work social security benefits to make the individual competitive.

We must also reiterate the changing role of government. Now, government merely persuades, rather than obligates, receptive employers to take on disabled people. Responsibility for ensuring that employers' practices do change is being devolved to employers' organisations and forums on the one hand, and to disabled individuals with grievances on the other. Anti-discrimination laws may make employers wary of being found guilty, and so reexamine their recruitment and employment practices. But if such policies are policed only by the individual, there will be less incentive to change. The statutory Code of Practice does not mean that practices will be overseen. An alternative threat is damage to an employer's image (and profits) through being branded a bad employer, as opposed to a 'good' employer who is 'positive about disabled people'. The Employers Forum on Disability 'peer group pressure' may pay off, but SMEs practices are likely to remain untouched. The Trades Union movement to date has had little impact on practices.

Our review of policies for disabled people in 15 countries (Lunt and Thornton, 1993) found that most governments had moved away from paternalistic state intervention to policies that encourage independence and individual responsibility. Observable in some European countries were attempts to shift the obligation for the employment of disabled people into the economic domain, as distinct from the state's, and to develop partnership with employers, employees and organisations of disabled people. In that context, the UK has a strictly limited concept of social partnership in the implementation of policy for the employment of disabled people.

9.1 Looking Ahead

Currently, neither major political party has well-developed plans for future disability employment measures, other than Labour's general commitment to strengthening the DDA. The Commission on Social Justice, set up by the last Labour Party leader, commented favourably on USA experience with contract compliance and advocated its use throughout the public sector (Commission on Social Justice, 1994).

Apart from campaigning for 'full civil rights', the disability movement has no coherent plan. A proposal for employment equity legislation was submitted by BCODP as written evidence to the House of Commons Employment Committee Inquiry, 1994. Companies over a certain size would have an obligation to register their equal opportunities policies and monitor their practices. An annual statement might include targets for recruitment and retention. Difficulties would be noted so that advice could be given. Such a legal document would be open to public scrutiny. BCODP suggested enforcement by withdrawal of permission to register, followed by a period for improvement. Failing that, the company would be fined and publicly de-registered.

In Canada, the general view of legislators has been that voluntary compliance with the Federal Employment Equity Act 1986 is likely to be more easily achieved than through punitive measures. Despite the limitations to the legislation, it serves to measure practice and, as the banks and communications media covered are highly visible, the action they take to remove barriers or improve opportunities serves to heighten awareness (Neufeldt and Friio, 1995).

Practices may be monitored from within the organization, as well as from without. With the shift from public towards increased private responsibilities, and a corresponding shift in the balance of power, it has been argued that there may be a new role for the 'consumers' of employment (Strümpel, 1995). While the UK is witnessing the emergence of a user movement of disabled people in the field of community care, there are no signs of a similar movement in employment.

The UK disabled people's movement has rarely addressed employment practices within their social model of disability (Lunt and Thornton, 1994; Thornton and Lunt, 1995). Barnes is one of the few disabled writers to emphasise tackling the workplace and the social organisation of work. Rejecting supply side policies, he advocates policies focusing primarily on the demand side of labour, namely on the workplace: 'policies creating a barrier-free work environment and requiring employers to use production processes accessible to the entire workforce, policies aimed at the "social organisation of work"' (Barnes, 1991, p. 97).

Such demand-side policies are insufficient in themselves. The reintegration of partially disabled workers requires jobs, at wage levels which can support them and their households.

References

Barnes, C., Disabled People in Britain and Discrimination: A case for Anti-discriminatory Legislation, Hurst and Co/University of Calgary Press, London, 1991.

Beinart, S., P. Smith and K. Sproston, K., The Access to Work Programme: A survey of recipients, employers, employment service managers and staff, Social and Community Planning Research, London, 1996.

Dench, S., N. Meager and S. Morris, S., The Recruitment and Retention of People with Disabilities, Institute of Employment Studies Report 301, Institute of Employment Studies, Brighton, 1996.

Department for Education and Employment, Disability Discrimination Act 1995: Code of practice for the elimination of discrimination in the field of employment against disabled persons or persons who have had a disability, London, HMSO, 1996.

Employment Department, The United Kingdom Response, response by the United Kingdom Government to the European Commission's Green Paper on European Social Policy, Employment Department, London, 1994.

Leichsenring, K. and C. Strümpel (Eds.), Mandatory Employment or Equal Opportunities? Employment Policies for People with Disabilities in the UN-European Region, Social Report No. 55, European Centre for Social Welfare Policy and Research, Vienna, 1995.

Lonsdale, S., C. Lessof and G. Ferris, Invalidity Benefit: A survey of recipients, Department of Social Security Research Report 19, HMSO, London, 1993.

Lunt, N. and P. Thornton, Employment Policies for Disabled People: A review of legislation and services in fifteen countries, ED Research Series No. 16, Employment Department, Sheffield, 1993.

Lunt, N. and P. Thornton, Disability and employment: towards an understanding of discourse and policy, Disability & Society, 1994, 9, 2, p. 223-238.

Maginn, A. and N. Meager, Local Employer Networks on Disability: Summary report, Brighton, Institute for Employment Studies, 1995.

Morrell, J., The Employment of People with Disabilities: Research into the policies and practice of employers, Research Paper No. 77, Employment Department, London, 1990.

Neufeldt, A. and S. Friio, Rights, equity and employment of disabled persons in Canada, in: K. Leichsenring and C. Strümpel (Eds.), Mandatory Employment or Equal Opportunities? Employment Policies for People with Disabilities in the UN-European Region, Social Report No. 55, European Centre for Social Welfare Policy and Research, Vienna, 1995.

Prescott-Clarke, P., Employment and Handicap, Social and Community Planning Research, London, 1990.

Rowlingson, K. and R. Berthoud, Evaluating the Disability Working Allowance: First findings, Policy Studies Institute, London, 1994.

Rowlingson, K. and R. Berthoud, Disability, Benefits and Employment: An evaluation of the Disability Working Allowance, Department of Social Security Research Report No. 54, The Stationery Office, London, 1996.

Sly, F., R. Duxbury, and C. Tillsley, Disability and the labour market, Labour Market Trends, 1995, December, p. 439-459.

Strümpel, C., Mandatory employment or equal opportunities? Summary of discussions, in: K. Leichsenring, and C. Strümpel (Eds.), Mandatory Employment or Equal Opportunities? Employment Policies for People with Disabilities in the UN-European Region, Social Report No. 55, European Centre for Social Welfare Policy and Research, Vienna, 1995.

Thornton, P. and N. Lunt, Employment for Disabled People: Social obligation or individual responsibility?, Social Policy Report Number 2, Social Policy Research Unit, York, 1995.

Thornton, P. and N. Lunt, Employment Policies for Disabled People in Eighteen Countries: A Review, Social Policy Research Unit, York, 1997.

Thornton, P., R. Sainsbury, and H. Barnes, Helping Disabled People to Work: A cross-national study of social security and employment provisions, Social Security Advisory Committee Research Paper 8, The Stationary Office, London, 1997.

Endnotes

1. The Act introduced the first comprehensive framework for the employment of disabled people. It provided for the setting-up of a disabled persons employment register; assessment, rehabilitation and training facilities; a specialised employment placement service; a duty on employers of 20 or more workers to employ a three per cent quota of registered disabled people; protection against unfair dismissal of registered disabled people; designated employment; and a National Advisory Council and local Advisory Committees.

2. A similar income supplement for low paid 'families without dependent children' has been piloted.

123

3. The Supported Employment Programme, which encompasses sheltered workshops and supported placements, placement, provides around 22,000 jobs. In March 1995, 45 per cent of those jobs were in supported placements.
4. Walking, climbing stairs, sitting, standing, rising from sitting, bending and kneeling, manual dexterity, lifting and carrying, reaching, speech, hearing, vision and continence. Susceptibility to fits is also scored. The mental health assessment covers ability to complete tasks, cope with daily living, deal with other people and cope with pressure.
5. Severe Disablement Allowance and the disability premium with Income Support (ISdp).
6. For an full account of measures in Australia, Canada and the USA, see Thornton and Lunt.

A Cross National Comparison of Disability Policies: Germany, Sweden, and the Netherlands vs. the United States

Leo J.M. Aarts, Richard V. Burkhauser and *Philip R. de Jong*

1 Introduction

Far too many people rely on social benefits, while too few citizens are at work contributing to economic growth and the financing of social welfare expenditures. The benefit rules and the high levels of taxation required to finance the system affect human motivation in a negative way and may increase the propensity to work unofficially in the 'black economy' (Swedish Ministry of Finance, 1994, p. 7).

Few people who have listened to the debate surrounding the passage of the 1996 welfare reforms in the United States, which are supposed to 'end welfare as we know it,' will be surprised by the language in the preceding quote. What may be more surprising is that it comes from a blue ribbon report to the Swedish Ministry of Finance entitled 'Social Security in Sweden – How to Reform the System'. Sweden, like most other Western European nations in the 1990s, has elected legislative majorities pledged to fundamentally reevaluate their traditional social welfare policies. The loss of productivity and the growing tax burden that are by-products of large social welfare systems are gradually eroding their popular support in European countries. While social equity is still a major goal of public policy in these countries, the real social costs of achieving this goal are now so high that even traditional supporters of the welfare state have begun to call for reform.

Countries like Sweden and the Netherlands, which were once looked upon as models of the modern democratic welfare state, now acknowledge that more of the same is no longer possible. Germany, struggling to economically integrate the eastern states that were politically integrated in 1990, has also joined the countries of Europe that are restructuring their social welfare systems. All three countries have experienced unprecedented post-war levels of transfer dependency and slow growth in the 1990s, and all three are attempting to come to terms with the competitive pressures of a single European market and the budget deficit restrictions that European Union members must meet to satisfy the requirements for entry into the Single Currency Union in 1999.

To the social, economic, and fiscal, pressures that are common to Sweden, the Netherlands, Germany, and the United States, must be added the less immediate but very real presence of aging populations. The aging baby boomers in each of these countries add a major long-term dimension to the growing public debate on the need to make existing social welfare systems more sustainable. In each country, changes in disability policy and the programmes that it encompasses have been at the centre of this debate.

In this book we first provide measures of the relative importance of disability policy in the Netherlands, Sweden, and Germany compared to the United States, and each country's reliance on transfer programmes to support people with disabilities who do not work relative to work-based programmes aimed at keeping people with disabilities employed. We will then provide a broader context from which to view disability policy and the current wave of reforms that appear to be leading to a convergence of disability policies across the four countries.

2 A Cross-National Comparison of Disability Transfer Populations

Table 1, derived from Aarts, Burkhauser, and De Jong (1996), suggests that economic and political forces play an important role in determining the relative size of the disability transfer population and how it changes over time. This table shows the ratio of disability transfer recipients per thousand workers by age over the past quarter century in the United States, the Netherlands, Sweden, and Germany. All four countries have experienced growth in this ratio since 1970, but the initial starting points and the patterns of growth are different, and these cross-national differences cannot be explained by differences in underlying health conditions in the four countries.

Table 1. Disability transfer recipients per thousand active labor force participants by age; unemployment rates; older male labor force participation rates, in four OECD countries, 1970-1994.[a]

	1970	1975	1980	1985	1990	1994
15 to 44 years						
The Netherlands	17	32	57	58	62	66
United States	11	17	16	20	23	38
Germany[b]	7	6	7	8	5	5[c]
Sweden	18	20	19	20	21	27
45 to 59 years						
The Netherlands	113	179	204	305	339	289
United States	33	68	83	71	72	96
Germany[b]	75	64	84	103	75	80[c]
Sweden	66	95	99	108	116	143
60 to 64 years						
The Netherlands	299	437	1033	1283	1987	1911
United States	154	265	285	251	250	294
Germany[b]	419	688	1348	1291	1109	1064[c]
Sweden	229	382	382	512	577	658
Total Population 15 to 64 years						
The Netherlands	55	84	138	142	152	151
United States	27	42	41	41	43	62
Germany[b]	51	54	59	72	55	54[c]
Sweden	49	67	68	74	78	97
Unemployment Rate						
The Netherlands	1.0	5.2	6.0	10.6	7.5	7.2
United States	4.8	8.3	7.0	7.1	5.4	6.0
Germany[b]	0.6	3.6	2.9	7.1	4.8	6.9
Sweden	1.5	1.6	2.0	2.8	1.3	8.0
Labor Force Participation Rates (x100) for Males, aged 55 to 64						
The Netherlands	81	72	63	47	46	43
United States	81	76	72	68	68	67
Germany[b]	80	70	67	60	58	50
Sweden	85	82	79	76	75	73

[a] Data are updates from Aarts et al. (1992).
[b] German data refer to the former Federal Republic.
[c] Figure refers to 1993.

127

In the United States the 52 percent increase in the relative disability transfer rolls in the 1970s was the result of both substantial increases in real social security benefits and the easing of eligibility standards for older workers. It was among those aged 45 and over that the ratio grew most rapidly (see Burkhauser and Haveman (1982) for a discussion of this period of disability policy history). Only the Netherlands had a comparable overall increase in its relative transfer population. In the United States, the political responses to programme growth of this magnitude were both the introduction of a stricter set of eligibility criteria and more vigorous enforcement of programme rules. The political backlash caused by the heavy-handed enforcement of these new rules led to a substantial relaxation in programme rules in the mid-1980s. A strong economy over the rest of the decade postponed the inevitable growth in the rolls due to these changes, so that by 1990 the relative disability transfer population was only slightly greater than it had been at the start of the decade. However, the pattern of programme growth in the United States over the 1980s was much different from that in the 1970s and signaled an important change in the characteristics of the new disability transfer population.

In the 1970s the United States joined the Netherlands, Sweden, and Germany in using its disability transfer system to provide early retirement benefits for older workers with health conditions that affected their ability to work, but who were not yet old enough to be eligible for benefits through the traditional social security retirement system. The growth in disability transfer rolls in Germany and Sweden during the 1970s was almost completely confined to workers aged 45 and over. Only in the Netherlands were workers under the age of 45 a significant component of the disability transfer population. The use of disability transfers as a bridge to early retirement in the United States is consistent with the creation of the Social Security Disability Insurance (SSDI) in the 1950s as a programme limited to older workers. Retrenchment in United States disability policy in the early part of the 1980s together with a strong economy in the remainder of the 1980s led to a mere 5 per cent increase in the relative disability transfer population during the decade. This was the smallest growth among the four countries shown in Table 1. But this small increase in overall growth conceals a 44 per cent increase in the relative disability population aged 15 to 44, an increase that far exceeded that of younger workers in the other countries. This increase put the United States ahead of Sweden and Germany in the use of disability transfer recipients per worker over this younger age range even though the United States was well below these two countries in overall disability transfer prevalence rates.

Propelled by the economic recession of the early 1990s in the United States, the relative disability transfer population aged 15 to 44 rose by 65 per cent between 1990 and 1994, and the overall relative disability transfer ratio rose by 44 per cent. This is in sharp contrast to what was happening in the other countries. Over these same early years of the 1990s, the ratio of transfer recipients per active worker actually fell in both the Netherlands and Germany. Only in Sweden did the ratio rise, but at about one-half the overall rate increase in the United States. Hence, by 1994 not only did the overall ratio of transfer recipients per worker in the United States exceed that of Germany, but for persons aged 15 to 44 the use of disability transfers in the United States was now substantially higher than in either Sweden or Germany. Only the Netherlands had a higher ratio of disability transfer recipients per worker among the younger population. Clearly the 1990s have seen a convergence in the prevalence of disability transfers as the welfare states of Europe struggled to reduce their disability transfer populations and the United States substantially added to its disability transfer population.

Three changes in the United States' disability policy rules prior to the recession contributed to this upsurge. First, the definition of mental impairment necessary to receive benefits was loosened. Second the requirement that the federal government show proof of medical improvements in a beneficiary's condition before benefits could be terminated were put into place in the mid-1980s. Finally, Supplementary Security Income (SSI) – a means tested welfare programme for those who do not qualify for Social Security Disability Insurance – eligibility criteria for children were loosened as a result of the 1990 Supreme Court decision in *Sullivan* v. *Zebley*.

These administrative and court enforced changes in United States Social Security regulations have dramatically altered the disability transfer system's population and its traditional role as a bridge to early retirement benefits for older workers. The massive increase in the numbers of SSI-children programme beneficiaries and the sharp increase in the number of younger beneficiaries on both SSI and SSDI have increasingly moved the United States toward the forefront of countries using disability transfers to provide income support to younger people.

Table 2 provides an alternative aggregate measure of the importance of government disability policy. It shows the share of Gross Domestic Product directly spent on disability transfer and work-based programmes by governments in the United States, the Netherlands, Sweden, and Germany. In 1991, the share of Gross Domestic Product (GDP) spent on people with disabilities through the public sector in the United States was small compared to Sweden, Germany, or the Netherlands. In the modern welfare states of Sweden and the Netherlands public expenditures on work-related and cash transfer programmes for people with disabilities were 4.08 and 5.24 per cent of GDP respectively. In Germany 2.22 per cent of GDP was spent on such programmes, while in the United States it was less than 1 per cent.

Table 2.   Public expenditure on labour market measures for the disabled, and on cash
benefits, as a percentage of GDP, 1991

	Vocational Rehabilitation	Direct Job Subsidies	Transfer Benefits
The Netherlands	(a)	0.64	4.6
United States	0.05	(a)	0.7
Germany	0.13	0.09	2.0
Sweden	0.10	0.68	3.3

(a) Less than 0.01 percent.

Source: OECD (1992), OECD (1993), Tweede Kamer der Staten-Generaal (1994), authors'
calculations.

But while a greater share of GDP was spent on both work and transfer programmes
in these European countries than in the United States, the United States spent the
largest share of its total programme budget on transfers and, hence, the smallest share
on vocational rehabilitation or direct job subsidies. The increasing upsurge in
disability transfer spending since 1991 is likely to make this emphasis on transfers
even more pronounced in 1996.

3 Placing Disability Programmes within the Broader Social Welfare System

To understand how disability policy varies across the countries we have been
describing, it is useful to look at these policies in a broader context. Disability
programmes are only one part of a social welfare system that attempts to ameliorate
the consequences of a separation from the labour market over a worker's lifetime for
economic as well as health reasons. These programmes can influence the response
of both employers and workers, when such a separation is imminent.
Figure 1 illustrates various government policies to ameliorate job loss caused by
economic or health factors as a series of paths that workers may take as they move
from full-time work to normal retirement.

130

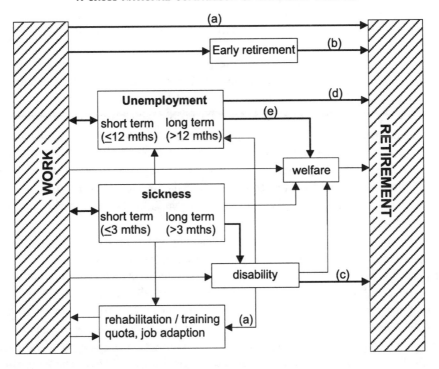

For workers who remain on the job all their work life the path to retirement is straightforward. Not until they reach early retirement age do they have to choose between retirement and continued work. But for a significant number of workers, job separation before retirement is a reality which social welfare policy must anticipate. To put Figure 1 into proper perspective, it is useful to recognize that the typical working-age (aged 15 to 64) person with a disability was able-bodied during most of his or her lifetime. For instance, for the United States, Burkhauser and Daly (1996) find that, in 1992, 70 percent of men and women aged 51 to 61 who reported having a health-related impairment said it started during their work life. Hence, the social welfare policy of the country can influence whether such workers remain in the labour force or end up in some form of transfer programme. Figure 1 illustrates five paths that workers may take following the onset of a health-related impairment. The *early retirement path* (a) encompasses public and private provisions that allow workers to retire prematurely. Since the end of the 1970s these provisions have become immensely popular and, together with disability insurance, account for the decrease in labour force participation at older ages reported in Table 1. When early retirement schemes are actuarially fair, they are neutral with respect to the financial inducement to retire. But in general, such schemes are not neutral and instead encourage workers to retire early. But they allow workers with some health

131

conditions to exit from the labour market without going through the formal health path.

The *work path* (b) encompasses public programmes that provide or encourage rehabilitation (either publicly or privately provided) to overcome the work limitations caused by a disability. It also includes more direct labour market intervention through the creation of specific government jobs for people with disabilities, subsidies to those who employ such workers, job quotas, and job protection legislation-dismissal rules, *et cetera*, or general anti-discrimination legislation requiring accommodation for workers with disabilities. These policies attempt to maintain those with disabilities on the job and in the labour market, either through the carrot of subsidies or the stick of mandates. As we have seen in Table 2, the United States makes the least use of government expenditures in this regard.

The *health path* (c) encompasses traditional disability insurance based transfer programmes. This may include short-term programmes that mandate employers to replace lost wages during the first few weeks of sickness or to directly provide such replacement through short-term social insurance. In all European countries, this would include providing health care at no marginal expense to the worker. In the United States the provision of health care and short-term sickness benefits is determined through private contracts between employers and employees with only limited government regulation over terms and conditions of those contracts. After some point, workers are then eligible to move to a long-term disability insurance programme, which often requires meeting both health and employment criteria. This path eventually merges with the social security retirement programme. In European countries, like Sweden, the decision to encourage workers onto the long-term disability transfer programme or the work path is decided by more coordinated procedures than in the United States, where there is almost no coordination between government agencies providing disability transfers and those providing rehabilitation or training.

The *unemployment path* (d) encompasses short-term unemployment benefits to replace lost wage earnings due to cyclical economic downturns. At some point longer term unemployment insurance is made available, often at a lower replacement rate. Eventually, this also merges with the social security retirement system. Disentangling exits from a job because of a health condition and exits from a job because of economic forces is in practice a difficult and often controversial task, especially as these exits are influenced by the rules established by a country's social welfare system.

The *welfare path* (e) encompasses the set of means-tested programmes which serve as a safety net for those workers without jobs who are not eligible for health- or unemployment-based social insurance programmes. Welfare programmes can be universal, subject only to a means test and/or linked to an inability to work either because of poor health, poor job skills, or child rearing responsibilities. This track can continue past retirement age for those few individuals who are not eligible for social security retirement benefits.

Choosing among Life Paths

When a health condition begins to affect one's ability to work, important job-related decisions must be made by both the worker and his or her employer. These decisions may be influenced by the social policies of the country. The worker will consider the relative rewards of continued movement along the work path versus entry onto an alternative path. In like manner, an employer's willingness to accommodate workers will also be influenced by the social policies within which the firm must operate.

In countries in which welfare benefits are low compared to disability transfers, where unemployment benefits are of short duration, and little is available in terms of rehabilitation and job protection, it is likely that the supply of applicants for the health path will be relatively large. This supply of applicants will increase as the replacement rate increases and as the period over which benefits can be received lengthens. In such a country, which describes the social welfare systems in the Netherlands and the United States, increases in applications for benefits put tremendous pressure on the disability system in times of serious economic downturns. Alternatively, when the protection offered by the unemployment path is similar to that offered by the health path, and minimum nonhealth-related social welfare is available as a universal benefit, as in Germany, much less application pressure is put on the disability gatekeepers during economic downturns. And in Sweden, where health benefits are even more generous than in the Netherlands, application pressure is less severe because all persons suffering a health impairment are required to receive rehabilitation. Following rehabilitation, it is government policy to provide jobs in the public sector if private sector jobs are unavailable. In Germany, a combination of mandatory rehabilitation and a quota system deflects much of the pressure on the disability system. (For a fuller discussion of the German and Swedish disability systems see Wadensjö and Palmer, 1996.)

We have used Figure 1 as a framework for discussing how the incentive structure inherent in a country's social welfare system influences the supply of disability candidates. But we can also use Figure 1 to describe the 'demand' for such candidates. To enter any of the five paths described in Figure 1, it is necessary to satisfy entry requirements. The entry rules for early social security retirement insurance programme benefits are usually straightforward. A worker must have worked in covered employment for a given time or have performed other easily measured activities (i.e. attended school, raised children) and must be a given age.

Such eligibility criteria are easy to administer. This makes the task of the front line gatekeepers routine. They simply follow relatively objective criteria with little room for individual interpretation.

Of course, the overall size of the population on the retirement rolls will change if a higher benefit is paid or the age of eligibility is lowered, but gatekeeper discretion will not enter into this change. Gatekeepers will simply follow new criteria. Determining eligibility for the various paths open to those who have a health condition that begins to affect their work but who are below early retirement age is not as clear cut.

Unlike age, disability is a complex concept that has both health and work-related components. In a search for easily measured screens for benefits, most disability benefit systems require a waiting period of around one year between the onset of the condition and eligibility. They also check how much the person is actually working. They then use evidence from either a private physician or a physician employed by the system to determine the seriousness of the health condition with respect to the person's ability to work. While the first two pieces of evidence are easily observable, the third is less so. Doctors can evaluate health conditions as they relate to a norm, but there is no unambiguous way to relate a health condition to ability to work. Hence, much of the problem with administrating a disability system is in establishing criteria for eligibility and developing procedures that will insure consistency in its use. Here, gatekeeper discretion in carrying out established criteria is much greater than it is for retirement.

Access to the work path and the health path may be closely coordinated, as in Germany and Sweden, where a centralized group of gatekeepers determines who is rehabilitated and who goes directly onto disability transfers. But these paths may also be administered in quite independent ways. In the United States, rehabilitation services are administered by a gatekeeper with little or no connection to the gatekeepers who administer the disability transfer system. And in the Netherlands the emphasis on income protection and the use of the disability insurance programme as an exit route minimalizes the supply of rehabilitation services despite signals of modest demand.

All of these factors affect the way in which frontline disability gatekeepers respond to changes in supply and to the voices of those at higher levels of administrative responsibility who are attempting to control the overall flow of people into the system. In periods of economic downturns the number of workers who leave their jobs rises and applications to transfer programmes increase. In countries like the United States and the Netherlands, with generous disability benefits relative to other alternatives, tremendous pressure is put on the disability system to provide income for those unemployed workers and their families. The pressure may lead to a specific

134

easing of the rules or simply to a change in the interpretation of the rules. In this way 'demand' may shift to accommodate supply.

4 A Comparison of Work and Transfer

In European welfare states, social insurance covers all employees against the risk of wage loss due to temporary sickness or permanent disablement. Sick-benefit usually covers all health contingencies, whether objectively assessable or not. If the disability has a work-related cause, a separate work injury programme may replace wage loss. European work injury plans are similar to the United States Workers' Compensation programme in both design and origin. Work injury programs were the first form of social insurance in all early market economies.

In almost all welfare states, coverage of work injury and related risks is compulsory for private employment. One of the exceptions is the Netherlands, which abolished the distinction between work-related and other causes of disability under its disability insurance scheme in 1967.

Most disability transfer programmes covering social risks, e.g., nonwork-related contingencies, consist of an employment-related social insurance scheme and a separate arrangement for disabled persons with little or no work experience. In the Netherlands and Sweden, compensation for loss of earning capacity due to long-term impairments is provided by a two-tier disability insurance programme. The first tier is universal, with eligibility being based on citizenship. These national disability insurance programmes typically offer flat rate benefits that are earnings tested. They target those disabled at birth or in early childhood and provide benefits from 18 years onwards. In the Netherlands, these basic benefits also cover self-employed people. In Germany, employees who become disabled before their 55th birthday enjoy entitlements as if they had worked until they reach 55.

Eligibility for a supplement is restricted to labour force participants. These second-tier benefits are based on age or employment history and wage earnings. In Germany, Sweden, and the United States, an earnings-related disability insurance programme is part of the legal pension system. Coverage depends on contribution years. More specifically, at least three years (Sweden) or three out of the five years (Germany) preceding a contingency must be spent in paid employment. Wage earners are obliged to participate, and the self-employed may participate voluntarily. The Netherlands has no contribution requirement for earnings-related benefits in terms of years of covered employment, but in 1993 they introduced a system of age-dependent supplemental benefit sizes that simulate a contribution years requirement.

5 Eligibility Requirements and Benefit Levels

By definition, eligibility for disability pensions is based on some measure of (residual) capacity or productivity. Germany has a dual system: full benefits for those who lose two-thirds or more of their earning capacity with regard to any job available in the economy and partial benefits for those who are more than 50 per cent disabled with regard to their usual occupation. Under the Handicapped Act of 1974, workers with a permanent reduced labour capacity of 50 per cent or less are entitled to the status of 'severely disabled' (*Schwerbehinderte*). Workers are entitled to extra vacation and enjoy protection against dismissal. Although being recognized as a severely disabled worker does not give access to cash benefits, it allows one to retire at 60 with a full pension, given sufficient (15) contribution years.

Sweden has a more lenient eligibility standard. Capacity to work is measured with regard to commensurate employment instead of any gainful activity as in Germany and the United States. Moreover, the Swedish programme has four disability categories, depending on the size of residual capacity, with corresponding full and partial pensions.

The Dutch disability programme is unique in that it distinguishes seven disability categories ranging from less-than-15 per cent, 15-25 per cent disabled, and so on to 80-100 per cent disabled. The minimum degree of disability yielding entitlement to benefits is 15 per cent. The degree of disablement is assessed by consideration of the worker's residual earning capacity. As of 1994, capacity is defined by the earnings flow from any job commensurate with one's residual capabilities as a percentage of pre-disability usual earnings. The degree of disablement then is the complement of the residual earning capacity and defines the benefit level. Before 1994, only jobs that were compatible with one's training and work history could be taken into consideration. Since then, in an effort to reduce the flow of new entrants onto the disability rolls, not only has the definition of suitable work been broadened, but the medical definition of disability has been tightened, too. Under the new ruling, the causal relationship between impairment and disablement has to be objectively assessable.

6 Administration

The preceding short overview of 'the rules of the game' does not say much about how the game is played. It does not explain why different national schemes produce the divergent results seen in Tables 1 and 2. For instance, the disproportionate

136

disability transfer population in the Netherlands has more to do with the way in which the rules are applied than with the rules as such.

The Dutch disability plan differs from other national programmes. It has no separate work injury scheme and a more elaborate system of partial benefits. Furthermore, its social insurance programmes (disability and unemployment insurance, and sick-benefit) are run by autonomous organizations, which lack direct governmental (political) control. These organizations are managed by representatives of employers' organizations and trade unions. Membership of an employers' association is obligatory for every employer. The Industrial Associations have discretion to develop benefit award and rehabilitation policies without having to bear the fiscal consequences, as disability programme expenditures are funded by a uniform contribution rate. Thus, administrative autonomy is not balanced by financial responsibility.

In Germany and Sweden, disability insurance is part of the national pension programme run by an independent national board that is closely supervised by those who are politically responsible for the operation of the social security system and therefore subject to parliamentary control. These boards monitor disability plans and safeguard uniformity in award policy by issuing rules and guidelines to local agencies. The difference between these countries and the Netherlands, then, is that their disability systems are under some form of government budgetary control.

In the Netherlands, disability assessments are made by teams of insurance doctors and vocational experts employed by the administrative offices of the Industrial Associations. These teams also have to determine the rehabilitation potential of disability claimants and to rehabilitate those with sufficient residual capacities. A further potentially important difference from other European countries, then, is that the Dutch disability assessment teams are legally obliged to examine every benefit claimant personally, not just administratively. This may have spurred a liberal, conflict-avoiding attitude, especially since neither the gatekeepers themselves nor their managers are confronted with the financial consequences of award decisions. Sweden administratively checks disability claims by means of written, medical and other reports to prevent the programme gatekeepers from being influenced by self-reports and the physical presence of claimants. In Germany, too, award decisions are made using medical reports and applying uniform decision rules developed by specialists' panels, each covering a diagnostic group.

7 Disability or Unemployment?

Like other fringe workers, persons with disabilities have a higher-than-average sensitivity to cyclical downswings. Even in the absence of a disability transfer programme it is likely they would have a greater risk of job loss during recessions. European workers who lose their jobs are usually covered by unemployment insurance. Entitlement to earnings-related unemployment insurance benefits is of limited duration and is followed by flat-rate, means-tested social assistance. In the Netherlands, Germany, and Sweden, entitlement durations depend on age; workers older than 58 or 60 may keep unemployment insurance until they reach pensionable age (65) or qualify for disability insurance benefits on non-medical, labour market grounds. The use of disability benefits as a more generous, less stigmatizing, alternative to unemployment benefits was quite common in these countries between 1975 and 1990. It provided employers with a flexible instrument to reduce the labour force at will and kept official unemployment rates low. This approach was very popular in Sweden until 1992, when the law was changed and disability pensions based solely on unemployment could no longer be awarded.

The Netherlands had similar experiences. Until 1987, the law explicitly recognized the difficulties impaired workers might have in finding commensurate employment by prescribing that the benefit adjudicators should take account of poor labour market opportunities. The administrative interpretation of this so-called labour market consideration was generous so that it led to a full disability benefit to almost anyone who passed the low threshold of a 15 per cent reduction in earnings capacity. The share of unemployed or 'socially disabled' among disability insurance beneficiaries, applying the pre-1994 eligibility standards, is estimated to be 40 per cent (see Aarts and De Jong, 1992, 1996). The fact that the abolition of this legal provision could not halt the growth in the incidence of disability transfer payment recipients, as can be seen in Table 1, induced further amendments between 1992 and 1994.

Labour market considerations also influence disability determinations in Germany. In 1976, the German Federal Court ruled that if insured persons have limited residual capacities and the Public Employment Service is unable to find them a commensurate job within one year, they can be awarded a full disability pension retroactively. Because partial disability benefits are based on the availability of commensurate work, certified skilled workers may refuse any job that is not at least semi-skilled in nature. A semi-skilled worker must only accept unskilled jobs that are prominent in pay and prestige. Unskilled workers who are not eligible for a full disability pension must accept any job or resort to unemployment or welfare. These regulations, in combination with a slack labour market, have reduced the proportion of partial pensions from 30 per cent in 1970 to less than 5 per cent in the early 1990s.

Assessment of rehabilitative potential is the counterpart of disability assessment. To reduce the flow of workers onto long-term disability transfer programmes, impairments should be cured, or their limiting consequences corrected, as soon as possible. The ultimate goal of a vocational rehabilitation plan is work resumption. This involves more than treatment, training, and the provision of corrective devices. It also involves job mediators and employers. Swift rehabilitation and redeployment depend on the willingness of all these different actors to invest money, time, and/or effort to boost the employment possibilities of impaired workers. The job of some of these participants (doctors, ergonomists, job mediators) is to help people overcome their handicaps. For others – the impaired workers and their employers – it is to some degree a matter of choice, and hence of incentives, as to whether they engage in rehabilitative efforts.

As Table 2 shows, policies differ with respect to public spending on rehabilitative services and on employment programmes for disabled workers. Rehabilitative services consist of providing corrective devices such as wheelchairs, workplace accommodations, or seeing-eye-dogs and services such as training, therapy, counseling, or job mediation. Given the broad accessibility of health care in European welfare states, there are no serious financial impediments to obtaining medical rehabilitation. Nevertheless, over the past years, as part of the changes in their welfare programmes, Sweden and the Netherlands have introduced patient fees for an increasing number of health and rehabilitation services.

National policies also differ to the degree that they require rehabilitation efforts. Mandatory rehabilitation is a possible outcome of the disability determination process in both Germany and Sweden. Moreover, Germany has hiring quotas, stipulating that firms should employ a certain percentage of workers who are registered as handicapped. Dutch and Swedish civil law does not require quotas but does mandate firms to provide commensurate work to employees who have become disabled on their current jobs. These mandates in principle are more farreaching than the more modest mandates imposed on firms by the Americans with Disabilities Act in the United States.

8 Rehabilitation Services

In addition to cash compensation, Dutch disability insurance offers in-kind provisions covering job accommodation and training costs to promote the employment of impaired workers. But public rhetoric with regard to the provision of these types of subsidies far exceeds reality. As we indicated in Table 2, spending in this area was minimal in 1991. In 1993, spending on general accommodations at home as well as at work under the Dutch disability insurance programme amounted to 800 million guilders. Only 20 million guilders (2.5 per cent of such general accommodation expenditures and about 0.1 per cent of total disability expenditures) was used for vocational rehabilitation and workplace adjustment. The amount was low because few claims were filed. The rest was spent on provision for general daily activities (mobility, dwelling, etc.). On a per capita basis, Germany spends over 40 times more than the Netherlands on vocational rehabilitation. Beginning in April 1994 general daily activities were no longer provided by disability insurance but have been transferred to the jurisdiction of a new, locally administered, Provisions-for-the-Handicapped Act. The structural level of spending on work-related provisions is estimated to be around 80 million guilders (Tica, 1995).

Various aspects of the disability pension system reflect the German commitment to work. First, a relatively large amount of money is spent on vocational rehabilitation (see Table 2). Impaired workers are referred to rehabilitation by the adjudicators of either sickness insurance or disability pension systems, or by the local employment agencies. Furthermore, to encourage employment of disabled workers, the Handicapped Act subsidizes employer expenses related to job accommodations.

The Swedish Social Security Administration and its regional and local offices do not have their own rehabilitation personnel or facilities. Instead, they enlist the services of the various medical, vocational, and other professionals in this field. Each county has its own labour market board and special centres for vocational rehabilitation and guidance. The centres are operated by the National Labour Market Board through the county labour market boards. Some of them specialize in groups with specific disabilities. The labour market boards oversee more detailed examinations than are given at the employment offices, in order to determine the work capacity of people with disabilities and to provide general help in developing the capacities necessary to work. However, in most cases, specific occupational training for the disabled is provided under the same programmes that train people without disabilities. The labour market boards also oversee training for the non-disabled. The share of non-disabled receiving training has gradually increased over time and is now about 50 per cent of all those being trained.

Recently, emphasis in Sweden has been put on early intervention for those receiving sick-benefit and on coordinating all parties involved in rehabilitation, i.e. medical professionals, unions, employers, company doctors, vocational professionals, and employment service administrators, as necessary. New legislation gives the social insurance offices the responsibility for initiating and coordinating rehabilitation. This has enabled social insurance administrators to act more like private insurers with a responsibility to contain costs. The government has established cost-reduction goals for all the regional offices regarding sickness and disability payments. In sum, the trend of recent years has been to make more resources available for rehabilitation, while at the same time to set goals.

9 Employment Policies

Provision of jobs for workers with disabilities can take several forms. One is job creation in the public sector, either as part of an employment policy targeted at the broader unemployed population or via a targeted approach of sheltered workshops for those with disabilities. Another way to promote employment is to provide wage subsidies to private business. Finally, employers may be forced to make room for disabled workers by regulations, such as requirements involving accommodation for recognized disabled workers, job protection, and employment quotas.

9.1 Sheltered Work

The Netherlands and Sweden have sheltered work programmes. The Netherlands has a national network of sheltered workshops, employing 88,000 people with a handicap (1.5 per cent of total employment). Sweden has 35,000 handicapped workers (0.83 per cent of total employment) in sheltered jobs. In both countries, the operating costs of these workshops are almost fully funded by government. On average, wages are higher than disability benefits, and part-time earnings may be combined with partial benefits. Work is not mandatory in either country.

9.2 Wage Subsidies and Partial Benefits

Apart from being an insurance device to compensate for the lost earning capacity, partial benefits also work as a wage subsidy. In fact, the introduction of the fine grid of seven disability categories under Dutch disability insurance was supported by explicitly referring to its rehabilitative aims when the programme was enacted in 1967. Partial benefits were intended to help disabled workers find commensurate employment. By liberal application of labour market considerations, it became routine to award full benefits under the presumption of a shortage of employment opportunities. This lenient approach was to have been changed by the 1987 amendments, which banned labour considerations assessing residual capacities. The old routines proved difficult to alter, however, and the amendments did not produce the expected results. At the end of 1995, 75 percent of current disability beneficiaries still had an award based on full disability. Hence, new cuts and changes were introduced in 1993 and 1994.

141

Like the Netherlands, Sweden and Germany have also seen a growing share of full disability benefits. Currently, 85 per cent of Swedish and 95 per cent of German beneficiaries (up from a 1965 low of 67 per cent) are labeled as fully disabled. In Sweden, a separate wage subsidy programme was introduced in 1980, replacing two earlier programmes. The compensation rate paid to the employer varies depending on the disability, on the duration of employment (compensation is generally higher in the first years after a person is hired; subsidies are not available for already employed persons), the sector in which the person is employed, and the person's age (compensation is highest for disabled youth). On average, the compensation rate was 73 per cent in July 1992 for those in their first year of support and 61 per cent for those assisted for longer periods. These wage subsidies are used by about 1 per cent of all workers.

9.3 Quotas

The German Handicapped Act requires that public and private employers with more than 15 employees hire one severely disabled person for every 16 job slots or pay a monthly compensation of 200 DM for each unfilled quota position. In 1990, approximately 900,000 severely disabled persons were employed, while 120,000 were unemployed. Despite the carrot of subsidies for workplace adjustments and the stick of monthly fines, in 1990, disabled persons made up only 4.5 per cent of the targeted work force, well below the 6 per cent quota. Only 19 per cent of the 122,807 public and private employers subject to the quota have managed to fill it; 44 per cent of these firms employ some severely disabled persons, although fewer than are required by the Handicapped Act. The remaining 37 per cent employ no disabled persons (Sadowski and Frick, 1996). While German authorities are rather critical of the effect of the Handicapped Act and compliance is far from full, the employment rate of disabled workers outside of sheltered workshops is high by international standards, even by comparison with Sweden.

Compliance with the German quota rules has declined steadily since 1983. The share of severely disabled workers in private sector employment went down from 5.4 per cent in 1983 to 3.6 per cent in 1994, while in the public sector it dropped from 6.5 per cent in 1983 to 5.2 per cent in 1994. Likewise, the unemployment rate among the severely disabled increased from 11.7 per cent in 1983 to 15.8 per cent in 1995. Or, in relative terms, the discrepancy with the total unemployment rate increased from 2.6 to 6.4 percentage points over the same 12-year period (Winkler, 1996).

9.4 Job Protection

Dutch legal regulations oblige employers to provide commensurate work to employees who have become disabled in their current jobs. After the onset of impairment, individuals can only be dismissed if continued employment in one's usual, or alternative, work would put an unreasonable strain upon the employer. An absolute dismissal ban is in force during the first two years of disability. After these two years the employer is usually granted permission to dismiss. Similarly, German workers who are designated as severely disabled have the right to demand workplace adjustments and enjoy protection against dismissal.

10 New Directions in Dutch Disability Policy

The disparity between the Dutch disability programme experience and that of the other countries may be largely explained by differences in incentive structures. Some of these incentives reflect national preferences. For instance, a strong preference for prevention and rehabilitation in Germany and Sweden has induced legislators to mandate rehabilitation for workers under the age of 60 with functional limitations unless they are 'severely' disabled. This policy is supported by a quota system in Germany, and by wage subsidies and employment programmes in Sweden. Such a policy gives a clear signal to the insured population that eligibility for disability transfer benefits is based on complete, and irreparable, loss of earning capacity. Likewise the United States' requirement of an, often uncovered, minimum period of five months without *any* gainful activity resulting from severe disablement, is meant to deter applications for a disability benefit.

Until the reforms of 1993 and 1994, such clear signals were missing in the Netherlands. In Germany, Sweden, and the United States, disability insurance is part of a national pension system that includes old age and survivors' benefits, for which entitlement is related to contributions paid. This pension system is administered by civil servants or local agencies under direct government control.

In he Netherlands, disability insurance is part of the system of employment based (wage-related) insurances, including sick-benefit and unemployment insurance, managed by the social partners. As mentioned before, these sickness and disability benefits became tools of workers and management to achieve outcomes that were not always in the national interest. Trade unions used the disability programme to guarantee generous and easily accessible transfer benefits to its members who no longer wanted to work or were unable to find work. Firms used these programmes to silently shed redundant workers. It was not until the end of the 1980s that the political process, which had relied upon consensus among the partners, began to unravel under the strain of the growing tax burden. International comparison of labour market and social security data, an increasing stream of private research, and several highly visible parliamentary investigations finally convinced the public and its legislators that using the disability insurance system as a pseudo-unemployment programme was fiscally and socially harmful.

In 1987, after prolonged public debate, the Dutch parliament enacted legislation to reform the system. Benefit levels were cut and a legal basis for disentangling the risks of disability and unemployment was introduced. But the 1987 social welfare reforms ultimately failed because they did not affect the incentive structure of employers and gatekeepers, and further adjustments were required. After a difficult political process, in which Social Democrats and Christian Democrats – the traditional defenders of the autonomy of the social partners – suffered great losses, some of the residual weaknesses in the system were repaired in 1993 and 1994, at the risk of abandoning the decades old requirement of consensus among the social partners. These reforms provide both administrative and financial incentives to workers and firms to refrain from overuse of the disability transfer programmes by making eligibility standards more stringent and by more directly linking programme use to programme costs.

10.1 The Disability Insurance Changes of 1993

Since August 1993, disability is more strictly defined, and the disability status of all beneficiaries who in 1993 were younger than 50 is being reviewed according to the new standards. These reviews affect almost half of the 1993 beneficiary volume and are scheduled to be completed by 1998. In 1994 and 1995, 91,500 beneficiaries younger than 40 were reviewed; 29 per cent had their benefits terminated, and 16 per cent were reclassified into a lower disability category with lower benefits (Ctsv, 1996a, p. 51). In 1994 alone, 52 per cent faced a termination (37 per cent) or reduction (15 per cent) of their benefits as a result of the reviews. A sample taken at the end of 1995 shows that one year after the reviews, 23 per cent of those 52 per cent who had suffered a loss of benefit income, had increased their work effort. More specifically, among those who were not gainfully employed at the time of the review, 30 per cent held a job one year later. Most of the others were still dependent on some form of transfer income (Ctsv, 1996b, p. 49-62). The reviews were successful in reducing the beneficiary volume, but less so in increasing the work effort of those who had a full award before they were reexamined using the stricter rules.

Under the new benefit calculations process enacted in August 1993 with the stricter eligibility standards, the disability benefit period is cut in two parts: a short-term wage-related benefit, with the previously existing 70 per cent replacement ratio, followed by a benefit with a potentially lower replacement ratio. Both the duration of the wage-related benefit period, and the replacement ratio thereafter depend on one's age at the onset of disablement.

Those aged 32 and younger are not eligible for wage-related benefits; those aged 33 to 37 are entitled to a six-month period of wage-related benefits; those aged 38 to 42 to a one-year period of wage-related benefits; those aged 43 to 47 to a 1.5-year period of wage-related benefits; those aged 48 to 52 to a two-year period of wage-related benefits; those aged 53 to 57 to a three-year period of wage-related benefits; those 58 and over to a six-year period of wage-related benefits. All of these periods are preceded by the existing 12-month waiting time covered by wage-related sickness benefits. During the follow-up period, a fully disabled beneficiary receives a base amount of 70 per cent of the minimum wage *plus* a supplement depending on age at onset according to the formula: [(age − 15) x 1.4 per cent] x [wage − minimum wage]. For beneficiaries with residual earning capacities, these replacement rates are adjusted in accordance with their degree of disability.

10.2 Forms of Privatization

These new benefit rules are a sharp break from a quarter century of disability entitlement to wage-related benefits of unlimited duration. Age now serves as a proxy for work history, or 'insurance years,' introducing a quasi-pension element into the disability system. The reduction in government-provided disability insurance has also spurred a lively market in which private insurers are competing with corporate and industry pension funds to cover the gap between the old and new systems. These supplements are financed by premiums that are differentiated according to risk at the level of individual workers or firms. Specific firms and even complete branches of industry signed collective bargaining agreements that readjust the gap between the old and new replacement rate so that, by 1994, 85 per cent of all employees were covered by such gap insurance.

Employers have shown a surprisingly strong willingness to purchase gap coverage. Apparently, their stated interest in reducing labour costs was outweighed by their desire to maintain a generous exit option for their redundant workers. The eagerness of private insurers to offer supplemental coverage is less surprising. After all, the new benefit calculation formula implies that younger and better paid workers face a lower replacement rate. In other words, groups with a low disability risk are hit hardest by these cuts. Under such favourable self-selection conditions, coverage of these cuts up to the original 70 per cent replacement, or even higher, is an attractive proposition for private insurers.

An additional form of privatization was introduced in 1994, when employers were mandated to cover the first weeks of sick pay themselves and to contract with a private provider of occupational health services to monitor sick spells, advise firms on the nature and extent of the health risks to which their manpower is exposed, and suggest ways to reduce these risks.

In March 1996, the Sick-Benefit Act was abolished and employer responsibility for coverage of sick pay was extended to a maximum of 12 months, after which Disability Insurance takes over. Apart from the obligation of firms to replace 70 per cent of earnings lost to sickness laid down in tort law, sick pay insurance is now completely privatized and firms may choose freely whether they want to bear their sick pay risk themselves or have it covered by a private insurer.

Plans to introduce experience rating in the calculation of disability insurance contribution rates and to allow firms to opt out of the social insurance system and self-insure their disability liabilities or have them covered by a private, for-profit, insurer are on the verge of being enacted. Also, introducing elements of experience rating into unemployment insurance are now being studied. All these changes are moving Dutch disability policy in the direction of assigning the costs of the programme to individual firms and workers more directly and away from the socialization of risks that dominated past policies.

10.3 Changing the Administration

In the debate on disability policy the focus gradually shifted toward the programme administrators. In 1992, the Dutch State Auditor (*Rekenkamer*) issued a report on the Social Security Insurance Council's supervision of Social Insurance administration during 1988 and 1989, the years following the 1987 Social Welfare Reforms. It concluded that the Social Insurance Council's supervisory performance had not been in conformity with the intentions of the legislature, and, furthermore, that the Deputy Minister of Social Affairs and Employment had failed to recognize this and to take proper corrective action.

In 1993, a multi-party parliamentary committee investigated the administration of the wage-replacing social insurance programmes, with special attention to the operation of the private employee disability insurance scheme. A vast number of current and former administrators, civil servants, and those politically accountable were publicly interrogated by the committee. The picture that emerged from the nightly televised summaries was devastating for the image of the Insurance Associations and the Social Insurance Council. What most suspected, and what had already been shown by research, was now publicly confirmed. The committee's report created broad

146

political support for drastic changes regarding, in particular, the dominant and autonomous position of the 'social partners' in the management of social insurance. Political pressure stirred up by public disclosure of the traditionally lax policy of the administrators has challenged gatekeepers to change their way of doing business. In addition, breaking the legally protected monopoly of the Social Insurance Associations over the administration and coverage of sickness and disability risks is likely to act as a brake on future excesses. Ministerial directives to apply the new, more stringent eligibility standards appear to be taking hold.

Evidence that the new rules are effective is that benefit terminations due to recovery, i.e. being found fit for generally accepted work, increased by about 40 per cent during 1994. Among the total population at risk, the incidence of new disability awards decreased by about 15 per cent in 1994; but among private sector employees they dropped by 25 per cent. At the same time, days lost to sickness also dropped by 15 per cent. While the disability benefit cuts have been offset to some degree by collective bargaining, supplements above the 70 per cent level have mostly been abolished. Therefore, the decrease in awards may well be the combined result of increased stringency of the gatekeepers and lower application rates.

A reduced number of awards and a sharp increase of benefit terminations resulted in a 2 per cent decrease of the private employee disability insurance beneficiary population in 1994. This was the first year in the history of Dutch disability policy in which the beneficiary population actually fell from the previous year. In 1995 the drop in the number of beneficiaries was even steeper: 6 per cent.

11 Conclusions

Our cross-national study confirms that incentives matter. Differences in institutional settings, and the incentive structure such settings imply, are a plausible explanation of the diverging trends and transfer levels of disability populations described in Table 1. These populations will be unnecessarily large unless the adverse incentives for employers and employees to use the disability transfer system as an alternative for rehabilitation or unemployment insurance are counterbalanced by administrative regulations or routines that either reduce the discretionary powers of individual employers and employees or provide contrary incentives. This is the lesson of the Netherlands. And it is a lesson that the United States should carefully consider as it ponders how to stem the rising tide of younger persons onto the disability transfer rolls.

Administrative organizations need standardized assessment and review protocols, the authority to enforce compliance with quota or other labour market regulations, and

147

the ability to prescribe and mandate rehabilitation. But the administration also needs the motivation to apply the available instruments adequately.

While private insurance carriers are motivated by a competitive market environment, public services require either bureaucratic control mechanisms or budget containment of some sort. In the four countries discussed here, disability insurance is publicly administrated, but there are significant differences in administrative design. In the United States government bears direct responsibility for the administration. Allocation of benefits is safeguarded by combining bureaucratic control with budget containment. In the Netherlands, on the other hand, until 1995 government had only indirect administrative responsibilities. Both the actual administration and its supervision and control were delegated to semi-public organizations run by the social partners. Bureaucratic controls were weak and budget containment mechanisms virtually non-existent. German and Swedish administrations are somewhere in between, Germany being closer to the Netherlands in allowing some influence from labour and management, but under much stricter government control. Sweden is closer to the United States, with benefits administered by government agencies and the social partners having a direct connection only to the provision of employment services. In both Germany and Sweden the administrative system is closely monitored by government to ensure that disability insurance is administered according to the public interest.

What seems clear from the experiences of Germany, Sweden, and the Netherlands is that, regardless of the administrative structure in which disability transfer programmes operate, partial benefits have only a limited impact. It is unclear to what extent factors such as labour market consideration or assessment problems make gatekeepers reluctant to award partial benefits, but in all three countries disability applicants are either declared fully disabled or rejected from the programme.

Currently, the Dutch administrative structure of wage-related public disability insurance is being dismantled. The reforms discussed in the preceding section have increasingly sought to privatize the system. These proposals have provoked a more fundamental discussion of the appropriate public-private mix in covering social risks. To strike a better balance between equity and efficiency, some form of 'managed competition' seems appropriate. The issue, however, of whether, and under what conditions, private carriers would be willing to provide coverage of the disability risk has not yet been spelled out. While it is far too early to tell whether the Dutch disability system has finally been brought under control, it is clear that many of the processes and policies that were responsible for its growth have been changed.

Social, economic, fiscal, and demographic pressures are all forcing changes in European social welfare systems that are moving them in the direction of a more actuarially fair but potentially more adversarial American style social insurance system. The main order of business for European welfare states today is to cut social expenditures and benefit dependency, and to increase financial support by promoting private employment. To the extent that this change in social policy is successful, it will lead to convergence in social welfare spending between countries like Sweden, Germany and the Netherlands, on the one hand, and poorer countries like Greece and Portugal which are still developing their social welfare programmes. Among the 12 countries that were members of the European Community in 1980, the coefficient of variation in social expenditures as percentage of GDP decreased from 0.28 in 1980 to 0.20 in 1993 – almost 30 per cent (Goudswaard and Vording, 1996). While social spending in all European Country member states (except Luxembourg) increased from 22.5 per cent of GDP in 1980 to 26.2 per cent in 1993, the drastic change in policies of comprehensive welfare states, like the Netherlands, may lead to an actual reduction of this GDP share, thus spurring further convergence. Because disability policy in the Netherlands has been a primary mechanism for increased social spending it has been the main target of reform by those who are attempting to bring social spending into compliance with the Single Currency Union guidelines.

Ironically, Dutch disability policy, which has been used as an example of what not to do in cross-national comparisons over the last two decades, may now be seen as the trend-setter among European countries in terms of introducing privatization of disability risks in order to achieve these Single Currency Union goals.

References

Aarts, L.J.M. and Ph.R. de Jong, Economic Aspects of Disability Behavior, North-Holland Publishing, Amsterdam, 1992.

Aarts, L.J.M., R.V. Burkhauser and Ph.R. de Jong, The Dutch Disease: Lessons for U.S. Disability Policy, Regulation, 1992, Vol. 15, No. 2 (Spring), p. 75-86.

Aarts, L.J.M., R.V. Burkhauser and Ph.R. de Jong, Curing the Dutch Disease: An International Perspective on Disability Policy Reform, Avebury, Aldershot U.K., 1996.

Aarts, L.J.M. and Ph.R. de Jong, Evaluating the 1987 and 1993 Social Welfare Reforms: From Disappointment to Potential Success, in: L.J.M. Aarts, R.V. Burkhauser and Ph.R. de Jong (Eds.), Curing the Dutch Disease, Avebury, Aldershot U.K., 1996.

Burkhauser, R.V. and R.H. Haveman, Disability and Work: The Economics of American Policy, Johns Hopkins University Press, Baltimore, 1982.

Burkhauser, R.V. and M.C. Daly, The Potential Impact on the Employment of People with Disabilities, in: J. West (Ed.), The Americans with Disabilities Act: Early Implementation, Blackwell Publishers, Cambridge USA, 1996.

Ctsv (College van Toezicht Sociale Verzekeringen), Augustus-rapportage, Zoetermeer, 1996(a).

Ctsv (College van Toezicht Sociale Verzekeringen), In en uit de WAO, Zoetermeer, 1996(b).

Frick, B. and D. Sadowski, A German Perspective on Disability Policy, in: L.J.M. Aarts, R.V. Burkhauser and Ph.R. de Jong (Eds.), Curing the Dutch Disease, Avebury, Aldershot U.K., 1996.

Goudswaard, K.P. and H. Vording, Is Harmonization of Income Transfer Policies in the European Union Feasible?, paper presented at the 52nd Congress of the International Institute of Public Finance, Tel-Aviv, 1996.

Ministry of Finance, Social Security in Sweden – How to Reform the System, Report to the Expert Group on Public Finance, Stockholm, 1994.

OECD, various years, Labour Force Statistics, OECD, Paris.

Tica, 1994 Jaarverslag (Annual Report) Algemeen Arbeidsongeschiktheidsfonds, Amsterdam, 1995.

Tweede Kamer der Staten-Generaal, Sociale Nota 1994, The Hague, 1994.

Winkler, A., Integration of Persons with Disabilities into the Labour Market and State Intervention, working paper, Centre for Labour and Social Policy, University of Trier, Germany, 1996.

Wadensjö, E. and E.E. Palmer, Curing the Dutch Disease from a Swedish Perspective, in: L.J.M. Aarts, R.V. Burkhauser and Ph.R. de Jong (Eds.), Curing the Dutch Disease, Avebury, Aldershot U.K., 1996.

Keys to Reintegration Facilitation: Persuasion as the Convincing Force

Stella den Uijl, Saskia Klosse, Tineke Bahlmann and *Joop Schippers*

1 Referential Framework

Now that we have obtained an overview of the situation in the various countries investigated, the question arises what conclusion we may draw as regards the factors that promote or hinder reintegration. An analysis of the policies conducted in the various countries firstly tells us that the degree to which certain factors either promote or hamper reintegration is to a large extent related to the choices a government makes as regards the distribution of responsibilities for the realization of reintegration of partially disabled people. A number of policy choices is possible in this respect.

A first option is to make the government primarily responsible for successful reintegration. More specifically this will mean that the government sees to it that a conglomerate of public services exists which together have the task of contributing to reintegration. Besides organizations charged with social security, one can also think of public health care organizations and employment offices or other employment intermediation organizations.
In this policy the responsibility for and the actual implementation of reintegration measures lies with these organizations and not primarily with the company or the partially disabled person himself. It is, therefore, called a government care policy.

Another option would be to allocate the responsibility for reintegration primarily with the employer (organizations) and trade unions and/or the partially disabled person himself. From the various contributions to this book we may deduce that this option can be realized in many ways. The decisive factor in this appears to be the extent to which the government furthermore decides to play an active role as regards reintegration promotion. In this context a number of different policies can be distinguished.

On the one hand there is the policy where the government keeps a rather low profile and leaves reintegration promotion mostly to the companies, or in other words, to the market. In this policy the role of the government is limited to taking statutory framework measures for reintegration with the tacit understanding that such measures must not hinder the free market. Consequently, the actual measures taken to promote reintegration usually are not of an obligatory nature. In this policy the company is not directly forced to contribute to reintegration. The emphasis is rather on voluntarily contributing to realizing reintegration at company level. More specifically this can take the shape of measures aimed at stimulating proper entrepreneurship. Reintegration policies structured according to these ideas will henceforth be referred to as market policies.

One may also opt for a policy of more obligatory nature. Reintegration promotion is then not left entirely to the free market. Instead the preliminary conditions are formulated in such a way as to demand cooperation in furthering reintegration at company level. In this policy the government plays a rather more active role in that it tries by means of statutory measures to stimulate employers into contributing more actively to reintegrating partially disabled people. Pursuant to the terminology used in Scandinavian countries, reintegration policies based on such ideas will hereinafter be referred to as work-line policies. Characteristic of such policies is that they aim primarily at achieving a more positive attitude among employers towards working with partially disabled people. This can be done either by means of indirect or more direct coercion.

Indirect coercion can be exerted by using negative financial stimuli for both the company and the partially disabled person himself. More specifically these would be stimuli such as fines imposed on employers or introducing an employer period, or sanctions such as withdrawal of benefits in case of non-cooperation with reintegration efforts.
Behaviour can also be influenced by means of positive financial stimuli. For the company these could take the form of labour cost subsidies, compensation for adaptation of the workplace and possibilities of trial placement. As regards the partially disabled person himself examples are training possibilities, and possibilities to gain work experience.
A clear example of measures involving more direct coercion is the introduction of a quota system. After all, employers are then under obligation to employ a certain percentage of partially disabled people.

2 Evaluation of the Developments in the Investigated Countries

2.1 Shift in Emphasis Towards Work-line Policy

Analyzing the policy choices made in the countries included in this study we learn that the responsibility for successful reintegration lay till the end of the 1980s in most countries with the government or the government and employers together, where the emphasis was on voluntary cooperation at company level in achieving reintegration. Though in some cases there is some degree of coercion in that there is a quota system, this usually takes the form of coercion combined with a certain degree of voluntariness. This is apparent in the fact that quota systems usually allow employers to buy off the imposed obligation by means of a pecuniary contribution.

During the Nineties the emphasis shifted in that there is now a clear tendency discernable to increase the responsibility of both the company and the partially disabled person himself. More than used to be the case they are asked to contribute actively to realizing reintegration. This means that in most countries emphasis shifts towards the work-line policy. However, there are some differences in how this policy is implemented and these will be discussed below.

2.2 Specification of the Work-line Policy in the Investigated Countries

2.2.1 Highlights of the Scandinavian Policy
In the Scandinavian countries the above mentioned trend has resulted in the government care policy losing significance. Even though the government institutions are still clearly responsible for the realization of the reintegration goal, employers are pressured more than used to be the case to retain partially disabled employees whenever possible.

To this effect Swedish employers, for instance, are obliged at an early stage of work incapacity to draw up a reintegration plan. Furthermore, they have to take measures to secure reintegration with another employer should they fail to relocate the disabled employee within their own company. In order to stimulate the partially disabled employee to assist in executing the reintegration plan the Swedish system furthermore provides for a reward in the form of extra, in-work benefits.

It must be noted that these measures aim at those who become partially disabled while employed by a company. As regards partially disabled persons outside the

153

labour market the responsibility of employers extends less far. The government (still) is primarily responsible for this group without an employer.

2.2.2 Highlights of the Dutch Policy

As in the Scandinavian countries in the Netherlands too there is a trend towards the work-line policy. Compared to the policy pursued in the Nineties this shift entails a change in that Dutch reintegration policy is now of a more obligatory nature, especially at company level.

Previously in the Netherlands, as was the case in Belgium, the emphasis was on voluntary contributing to reintegration promotion at company level. Article 2 WAGW (Employment of Handicapped Workers Act) which only provides for an obligation of effort in this regard, is a clear example thereof. Since the Nineties this emphasis has shifted particularly in the Netherlands towards a larger degree of coercion to actually meet this obligation of effort. Financial stimuli serve as a magic potion in this context.

The fact that this means has been chosen indicates that a choice has been made for measures influencing behaviour in order to achieve the goal set. Besides stimuli which aim to induce employers via a possible cost increase to actively contribute to successful reintegration, also positive financial stimuli have been introduced which are to help employers in a positive sense to accept their responsibilities in this matter.

The choice for this kind of indirect measures seems to indicate the conviction that the best results will be achieved especially by either positively or negatively stimulating the willingness of the parties involved to accept their responsibilities as regards reintegration.

2.2.3 Highlights of the German Policy

This 'stimulation' course deviates from the course set out in Germany. Here there has always been a tendency to opt for a larger degree of coercion in order to achieve reintegration of partially disabled people. This is apparant in among other things, the fact that in Germany (the only one of the countries studied here) there is still a quota system.

Studying the German system we learn that such a system is most effective in cases where someone becomes partially disabled while employed. Those who have no (longer) a labour contract appear to benefit very little by this system. This implies that employers are not or hardly affected by the existence of a quota obligation when hiring personnel. Rather, the existence of this kind of pressure seems to stimulate the use of the possibility offered by the quota system itself to shirk this obligation.

2.3 UK: A Separate Course

It can be said that the most obvious opposite of the German system is the reintegration policy pursued in the UK. Characteristic of that is that the realization of reintegration has recently been left primarily to the free market. The introduction of forms of coercion via measures imposed by the government is hard to reconcile with such a market policy. The emphasis therefore is on voluntary participation in the realization of reintegration by the employers (organizations) and the partially disabled people themselves. The free interaction of supply and demand is thus primarily decisive for the degree to which reintegration is actually acheived.

This does not mean that there is no form of supportive legislation at all. In the UK, however, this has been structured differently from the other countries that have been studied. Here namely anti-discrimination legislation is supposed to entice employers and partially disabled people to accept their responsibilities as regards reintegration. The key notion behind this is that if it is necessary to invest in reintegration promotion, this should primarily be done by promoting opportunities for individual competition. This has been concretized by conferring on individual disabled people the right not to be discriminated against and by persuading employers to make adjustments for disabled persons where it is reasonable to do so. Furthermore, disabled job-seekers are aided by training and in-work social security benefits to make them competitive. Thus it must be guaranteed that a partially disabled person is just as competitive as a healthy applicant and perforce have equal opportunities in the labour market.

This requires a different approach from that taken in the other countries included in this study. Under the British system namely disabled persons must be in employment or competing for a particular post before they can be protected. The basic assumption being that they are in principle able to meet the essential requirements for the job. Whether this approach will indeed result in reintegration depends to a large extent on whether the 'preparatory course' provides adequate education, training and support services to get disabled people in the position of being able to use the legal challenges. Furthermore, the attitude of employers towards partially disabled too plays a decisive role.

If one adds this to the fact that employers have no direct obligation to actually employ partially disabled people, it seems reasonable to doubt whether this system will prove adequately persuasive to achieve reintegration of partially disabled people. In view of the specific problems involved in realizing reintegration of partially disabled people the danger that the system will in the end succumb to its voluntary aspect, is quite real.

3 Decisive Factors

3.1 Degree of Influence on Reintegration Process

From the above we may deduce that since the Nineties most countries included here have opted for the work-line policy. Actually, the UK forms the only exception. After all, during the Nineties the choice made in the UK was to leave reintegration primarily to the free market. Apart from the possibilities for partially disabled people to increase their 'market value', the degree to which reintegration will be achieved therefore depends on the individual employer's attitude towards working with partially disabled people, with all inherent consequences.
In the other countries more government pressure is considered necessary to achieve reintegration. This is apparent in the supplementary measures taken which, with varying degrees of coercion, aim to convince employers and partially disabled people of their responsibilities as regards actual reintegration promotion.

In itself the latter method seems to offer more possibilities to achieve reintegration than the market policy as applied in the UK. An important factor in this is that under the work-line policy clear responsibility for successful reintegration is allocated to those who can actually and directly exert influence on the realization process. From the various contributions to this volume, however, it is clear that this, in itself, is insufficient.

3.2 Transparant, Well-Attuned Responsibilities Attribution

Analyzing the reintegration policies of the various countries included here, it seems justified to conclude that a transparant, well-attuned attribution of responsibilities among the parties involved in reintegration is a factor that must not be overlooked when implementing such a policy.
This is for example very clear in the Swedish contribution. There, after all, the work-line policy proves to be frustrated mostly by too vague a statutory description of the

employer's responsibility. In practice it then remains unclear how far the employer's responsibility stretches, what the means are he should use to meet his obligations and what constitutes failure.

The obstruction this causes as regards the realization of reintegration is worsened if at the same time the distribution of responsibilities between on the one hand the employer and on the other hand the administrative institutions involved also remains statutorily ambiguous. The partially disabled then runs the risk of getting lost in between and in the end the reintegration goal is not achieved.

So, apart from a clearly specified allocation of responsibilities the Swedish contribution also indicates the necessity of a proper balancing of responsibilities between all parties involved. Both factors can therefore be considered crucial supplementary conditions for a successful work-line policy.

3.3 Striking a Balance in Applying Financial Stimuli

The Dutch contribution shows us that applying financial stimuli does not per force lead to more responsible behaviour as regards reintegration. In order to achieve reintegration a first condition is to take care that the positive stimuli applied to induce the parties involved to behave more responsibly are not overshadowed or negated by concurrent negative stimuli applied to achieve the same change in behaviour.

If this means is chosen the necessity to strike the right balance between both types of stimulus too is a crucial supplementary precondition for a successful work-line policy. If this balance is not found there is a real danger that the positive stimuli are negated by the negative ones, resulting in the employers trying to shirk their responsibility rather than to accept it.

3.4 Willingness

The danger of risk avoiding behaviour is equally serious in cases where employers are forced by means of more direct measures to accept their responsibility as regards the realization of reintegration. The German experiences with the quota system, for instance, show this.

These experiences also show that another factor involved in achieving reintegration must be taken into account, namely the obvious lack of willingness on the part of the employers to cooperate in achieving reintegration. Other contributions to this volume too also include indications for this. It seems that this lack of willingness proves a serious impediment.

Research into the underlying cause of this impediment seems to indicate that the above mentioned lack of willingness is primarily the result of the prejudices of employers as regards the possible productivity of partially disabled people. There are also clear indications that this counts even more in case of partially disabled people who have no (longer) work. For partially disabled employees who still have a job employers seem inclined to try harder.

Besides the fact that the legal system leaves employers less discretion as regards this latter group, it also seems important that employers have more information about the remaining labour capabilities of these partially disabled and are therefore better able to estimate what they are really capable of. From this we may conclude that having some indication of what a partially disabled person is capable of will have a positive effect on the employer's willingness to accept his responsibility for successful reintegration.

This conclusion at the same time appears to present an explanation for the differences in position between partially disabled people still employed and those who are not (or no longer) employed. After all, most employers will have no idea of the labour potential of unemployed partially disabled people and legislation intended to stimulate employers to hire them is usually far less coercive. Assuming that employers must in the end be free to choose who they wish to hire, most governments opt for stimulation policies in relation to this group. Such policies intend to induce employers to choose a partially disabled person when hiring personnel.

3.5 Insecurity Reduction

However, it remains doubtful whether the above goal can be achieved by means of specific measures implementing a stimulation policy. Many of these measures primarily aim at making it financially interesting for employers to hire partially disabled people. It is doubtful though whether this takes sufficient account of the fact that many employers believe that hiring partially disabled people entails mainly risks and insecurity. This idea is not based solely on perceived strictness of job security legislation, but also (mostly) on the the above mentioned prejudices about what partially disabled people are capable of in terms of productivity. A negative perception of their motivation and their (increased) chances of sick leave may add to that.

When drafting reintegration policies all these aspects must be taken into account. More specifically this means that such policies will have to aim at least at preventing as much as possible any form of risk avoiding behaviour. Bearing in mind that such behaviour is based mostly on prejudices and a negative perception of the possible working capacity of partially disabled people it seems sensible to attribute priority to measures which will enable employers to sample and test the partially disabled's working capacity and productivity over a certain period of time and free of obligations. In that way employers will experience that hiring partially disabled people can indeed be profitable for the company.

3.6 Support Services

Structuring reintegration policy in the above indicated way actually amounts to implementing a 'service strategy', where counselling and (mutually) gleaning information by gaining experience form the most important pillars. In view of the fact that a reduced working capacity is often caused by a mixture of medical, social and labour market problems, a strategy built on these pillars seems indispensable to support employers in actually accepting their responsibility for the realization of reintegration.
More specifically this could be achieved by allocating certain support services to the employment intermediation offices. Main tasks of these services, where teams of professionals in the field of reintegration promotion closely cooperate, are to inform and counsel employers on reintegration promoting measures.

These are not necessarily new measures. For upon close consideration, it is not a lack of reintegration promoting measures that forms the impeding factor in the current system, but rather serious insufficient use because of the above mentioned reasons. The support services should counter this by drawing the employers' attention to the measures that may convince them that hiring partially disabled people is not per definition a risky and uncertain business.
One of these measures would be trial placement while receiving benefits as well as the possibility to temporarily employ partially disabled people via employment agencies. Both measures enable employers to experience during a certain period of time what hiring partially disabled people entails and thus to learn that this need not be hazardous or uncertain.

This kind of measure can of course be supplemented with measures who make such trial periods financially attractive for employers, for example in the form of wage costs subsidies, compensation of costs incurred by adaptation of the workplace or by granting dispensation of the employer period when hiring partially disabled people. Such measures further facilitate achieving the ultimate goal.

Taking account of the observed percieved strictness of job security legislation a flexible dismissal system could, as regards that same goal, provide relief too. This can be done by making dismissal possible in case the employer can prove that there are no (more) real replacement possibilities within the company and that replacement with another employer also is impossible. In other words, the employer must have sound reasons for dismissing a partially disabled employee.

In order to avoid the partially disabled's position being undermined by such a system it is important that strict criteria be imposed by means of which it can be ascertained that the employer has indeed sound reasons to dismiss the partially disabled employee. Again, the above mentioned support services could play an important supportive role in this context.

3.7 Preventing Long-Term Partial Disability

Aside from the above it is of major importance that attention be paid to the enhancement of equal opportunities for partially disabled people in the labour market. The contributions to this volume tell us that particularly their disadvantageous position in the labour market is an impediment to their return to work. As a rule this disadvantageous position is in its turn caused by the fact that many partially disabled people have been outside the labour process for a long time. This factor not only obstructs the return to work for the partially disabled person himself, but also strengthens the earlier mentioned prejudices among employers about the possible working capacity of partially disabled people.

In order to counter this aspect it is crucial to attribute highest priority to prevention of long-term disability. One important means with which to achieve this is the obligation to draft a reintegration plan as soon as possible after disability occurs. Thus, after all, requalification measures may be introduced as soon as possible that may close the gap between workplace requirements and remaining personal skills. The competitiveness of partially disabled people in the labour market can thus be increased. The earlier mentioned support services can play an important supportive role in this too.

This is even more the case if the employer states he cannot replace the partially disabled person within the company, and he can support this with sound arguments. It is then important that replacement with another employer is achieved as soon as possible. Support services can enhance this development not only by supervising the quick and adequate application of the requalification measures the partially disabled person requires, but also by convincing potential employers with adequate information that they choose wisely when employing the person concerned.

4 Conclusions

From the information supplied in this book we may conclude that the importance of measures which positively support the reintegration process cannot be overestimated. In stead of strengthening the point of view that hiring partially disabled people is primarily a risky and insecure business, these measures aim to convince employers by means of experience that partially disabled employees can indeed prove very valuable. One of the core problems from which many reintegration obstructing factors spring, can thus be overcome. In view thereof the conclusion seems correct that a crucial key to successful reintegration is the above described approach which is primarily based on persuasion.

This conclusion is no plea for a reintegration policy where voluntariness plays a main role. The above unmistakably indicates that some government interference is necessary in order to 'help' the parties involved in the reintegration process to accept their responsibilities in this matter. Apart from the necessity to clearly describe and attune these responsibilities, the above also tells us that this interference is more successful if structured by measures that are based on persuasion rather than on direct coercion or cost increases. The latter measures very easily lead to risk avoiding behaviour. Reintegration is then obstructed rather than facilitated.

It seems to be of the utmost importance to take these perceptions into account when structuring reintegration policies. If not, the danger is that the in itself positive tendency to promote reintegration, as we have observed it in the countries included in this study, will end in a farce!

Selected References

Elshoff, R.P.Th., Reïntegratie in perspectief, Tica symposium, Succesvol reïntegreren: kansen voor de toekomst, Tica, Amsterdam, 1995.

Fortuin, K., H. Swinnen & H. Weijnen, Arbeidsongeschiktheid en reïntegratie, Nederland en Europa, Nederlands Instituut voor Maatschappelijke Opbouw, 's-Hertogenbosch, 1990.

Nijhuis, F.J.N., Reïntegratiebeleid: meer dan herplaatsing!, Tica symposium, Succesvol reïntegreren: kansen voor de toekomst, Tica, Amsterdam, 1995.

Prins, R. & E.M.C. Meijerink, Reïntegratie-instrumenten in het buitenland, Vuga, 's-Gravenhage, 1997.

Thornton, P. & N. Lunt, Employment for disabled people, social obligation or individual responsibility?, Social Policy Research Unit, York, 1995.

Wevers, C.W.J., Research-nota reïntegratie-instrumenten, Vuga, 's-Gravenhage, 1997.

Zeitzer, I., Quality, effectiveness and efficiency of rehabilitation measures, ISSA, Study Group on Rehabilitation, Florence, 1994.

Appendix A

About the Authors

Leo Aarts studied Economics at Tilburg University and Groningen University. He received his doctorate at Erasmus University Rotterdam (1990). He is associate-director of the E.M. Meijers Institute of Legal Studies at Leyden University and teaches Law & Economics. His current research focuses on (the economic aspects of) the design and implementation of social security (disability) insurance programs. Occasionally, he acts as a consultant on issues of social (disability) policy to the ministers of Finance, Social Affairs, and Education, to political parties and to the labour union.

Tineke Bahlmann studied Business Economics at Erasmus University Rotterdam. In 1988 she received her doctorate for an intensive research about strategic reorientations during a crisis in six Dutch companies. She is parttime Professor in Business Economics at Utrecht University and director and professor of the Centre for Organizational Learning and Change at Nijenrode University. She advises organizations about organizational change processes and organizational learning, which are also her research topics. She is also an associate of the Netherlands School for Social and Economic Policy Research (AWSB).

Richard V. Burkhauser is professor of economics at the Center for Policy Research, the Maxwell School, Syracuse University. He received his PhD in economics from the University of Chicago. His has published widely on the behavioral and income distribution effects of public disability and pension policies.

Philip de Jong studied Econometrics at the University of Amsterdam and Economics at the Erasmus University Rotterdam. Since 1992 he is Professor Extraordinary of Economics of Social Security at Erasmus University Rotterdam and Senior fellow at the Leyden Institute for Law and Public Policy (Law Faculty, Leyden University). His present research focuses on social security and the labour market.

Asbjørn Kjønstad is Professor of Social Law at the University of Oslo since 1985. From 1986 till 1988 he was Dean of the Faculty of Law and member of the Board of the same university. From 1982 till 1990 he was chairman of the Royal Community on Social Security Law. Now he is a member of the Norwegian Academy of Science, Vice President of the European Institute of Social Security and

163

member of the Region Committee for Medical Ethics. His main field of research is Social Security Law, Medical Law and Tort Law.

Saskia Klosse obtained her degree in law at Utrecht University, where she also wrote and defended her thesis 'Menselijke schade: vergoeden of herstellen?' (1990), a study into rules and regulations concerning disability in the Netherlands and the Federal Republic of Germany. From 1985 to 1995 she worked as an Assistent Professor with the section of Labour and Social Security Law of the department ISEP of the Faculty of Law of Utrecht University. Since 1996 she is an Associate Professor with the same section. Besides, she is a deputy-judge with the sector of administrative law of the district court of The Hague and lectures on the theory of human damage at the medical faculty of the Caltholic University of Leuven.

Neil Lunt graduated in Politics from the University of Durham in 1990. He joined the Social Policy Research Unit (SPRU) at the University of York in 1992, after researching, mentoring and education policy at the University of Huddersfield. His research at SPRU included community nursing and charging for community care. With Patricia Thornton he has undertaken comparitive reviews of employment policies and services for disabled people and a review of disability benefits and employment in the United Kingdom. Since January 1997, Neil Lunt has been a lecturer in the Department of Social Policy and Social Work at Massey University, New Zealand, where he is continuing to research and write in the field of disability employment policies.

Erik Samoy studied sociology at the Catholic University of Leuven where he obtained his MA in 1974. Since 1988 he has been employed with the HIVA (Higher Labour Institute) of the same University and since 1992 he is also employed as a research fellow with the Sociology Department (section Sociology of Social Policy). His primary tasks encompass supervising and coordinating research (at the HIVA) on provisions for disabled people, preparing lectures on social policies, focussing mainly on sociology of handicaps and provisions for disabled people, and preparing a doctoral thesis on Belgian labour market policies concerning the disabled.

Joop Schippers studied Economics at Erasmus University Rotterdam, where he graduated cum laude in 1981. He works as an Associate Professor at the Economic Institute and the Centre for Interdisciplinary Research on Labour Market and Distribution Issues (CIAV) of Utrecht University. He also is an Associate of the Netherlands School for Social and Economic Policy Research (AWSB). His main field of research is labour economics, especially issues concerning labour market inequality between women and men. The latter theme was also the subject of his doctoral thesis (1987), a study on wage-rate differentials between men and women. From 1993 to 1997 he was also a member of the Netherlands National Council on Equal Opportunity (Emancipatieraad), where he among other things contributed to reports on the pension system and the future of the tax and social security system. Currently he also acts as vice-dean of the Faculty of Law of Utrecht University.

Patricia Thornton graduated in English from the University of Edinburgh in 1971. She left her first career as a civil servant to enter social policy research, completing a post-graduate course in social administration at the University of Liverpool in 1975. Since then she has worked mainly in university research institutes, joining the Social Policy Research Unit (SPRU) as a research fellow in 1987. Her main specialist areas have been community care for older people, public participation in planning and service delivery, and employment policies and services for disabled people. At SPRU she has managed a series of cross-national and United Kingdom studies on disability, employment and benefits systems and is co-ordinator for a study of job retention strategies for disabled workers under the auspices of the International Labor Organization (ILO).

Stella den Uijl studied Business Economics at the Free University Amsterdam. After her graduation in 1993, she started doing research for a doctoral thesis 'Rehabilitation of partially disabled workers in the workforce in various European countries; decisive factors seen from an international perspective'. Since 1997 she is Assistent Professor Business Economics at Utrecht University. She also is associated to the Netherlands School for Social and Economic Policy Research, Utrecht University.

Lotta Westerhäll has all her law degrees from the Law School at Lund University. She was Professor Dr. of Public Law at Uppsala University from 1986 till 1989, Professor Dr. of Social Law at Lunds University from 1989 till 1995 and Professor Dr. of Public Law, especially Social Law at Göteborg University from 1996. She is now Vice-Chancellor of the School of Economics and Law at Göteborg University, member of several Academics of Science and Research Councils in Sweden, chairman and member of three governmental committies and member of European and Swedish Research Networks in those research fields, which are her main fields, such as Social Security Law (both Swedish and European), Medical Law and Social Welfare Law.

Albrecht Winkler studied Business Economics at the Universities of Wuppertal, Loughborough (GB) and Trier, specializing in social administration and management. He currently holds a position as a researcher at the Centre for Labour and Social Policy, which is affiliated to Trier University. His work analyses employment policies for disabled people with a focus on alternative or transitional forms of employment that might facilitate re-integration into the regular labour market. He is also responsible for updating the computer-based documentation on literature about 'disability and work', which is published yearly by the Centre.

Appendix B

The Economic Institute

The Economic Institute / Centre for Interdisciplinary Research on Labour Market and Distribution Issues (CIAV) of Utrecht University concentrates on research in the field of *Labour market and social inequality*. The research involves questions like those concerning male-female differences with respect to labour supply and earnings, labour market segregation and the causes and consequences of labour market flexibility. The research program has labour economics as a point of departure, but aims explicitly at cooperation with researchers from other disciplines, like sociology, law and demografy, who also take an interest in labour market issues. Even though the research is being performed within a univeristi context and leans heavily on theoretical insights much attention is paid to policy issues. That is why most of the research combines theoretical questions with empirical studies.

During recent years the Institute has been involved with research for – among others – the Department of Social Affairs and Employment, The Department of Education, the (Dutch) Organisation for Strategic Labour Market Research (OSA), the Netherlands National Council on Equal Opportunity and the European Commission. Frequently grants are obtained from the Dutch Organisation for Scientific Research (NWO).

Staff from the Institute is involved in the supervision of several doctoral projects e.g. on the effect of taxes on women's labour supply, on the reintegration of partially disabled workers, on the effect of children on women's life time earnings, on work-family policies, on the careers of older workers, on the relation between the labour market and employer's market power in commodity markets, on the (changing) nature of labour contracts and on increasing labour market flexibility. The staff of the Institute also frequently participates in advisory boards and committees on labour market policy issues.

Visiting/mail adress:
Kromme Nieuwegracht 22, 3512 HH Utrecht, The Netherlands
Telephone: + 31 30 2537100, Telefax: + 31 30 2537131
E-mail: *Name*@POBOX.RUU.NL

Appendix C

The Netherlands School for Social and Economic Policy Research (AWSB)

AWSB as an interuniversity, interdisciplinary and thematically oriented initiative
The Netherlands School for Social and Economic Policy Research (AWSB) is an interuniversity and interdisciplinary research school, officially recognized by the Royal Netherlands Acadamy of Arts and Sciences (KNAW). AWSB has a guaranteed staff of 29 fulltime senior researchers, 6 post-doctoral positions, 4 international fellows and over 60 PhD-students (so-called AIOs). Within the Research School the faculties of Law and Social Sciences of Utrecht University, the faculty of Social Sciences of the Erasmus University Rotterdam, the Catholic University Brabant (Tilburg) and the Law Faculty of the University of Amsterdam jointly organize a post-graduate teaching programme. The institutes also collaborate in carrying out research on the changes affecting the Dutch 'welfare state'. Topics under investigation include the underlying legal, economic and moral principles and these principles' manifestations in relation to policy and practice within the labour market, and in terms of social provision.

The AWSB member institutes are the following:
- Utrecht/Law, Utrecht University Institute for Legal Studies (AWSB/SERB)
- Utrecht/Social Sciences, the Interdisciplinary Research Institute for Social Sciences, University of Utrecht (AWSB/Isor)
- Tilburg/Social Sciences, the Work and Organization Research Centre (AWSB/ Worc)
- Rotterdam/Social Sciences, the Rotterdam Institute for Sociotific Policy Research (AWSB/Risbo)
- Amsterdam/Law, the Hugo Sinzheimer Institute (AWSB/Hsi)

The purpose of AWSB
The central aim of the AWSB-programme is to chart the forms and the causes of the contemporary transformation of the Dutch welfare state in a European comparative perspective. What are its characteristics and how do socio-economic, legal, administrative and socio-cultural aspects interrelate? What social problems, what new identities and what problems of distribution will result? How do citizens, administrators, policy-makers and public and private organisations anticipate and react? The

programme's guidelines represent its greatest challenge, namely to integrate the relevant social, behavioural and legal disciplinary expertise available in the Netherlands into a multi-disciplinary perspective on the interconnected contemporary developments within the welfare state regime.

The research programme
The actual research within the School is done under the auspices of 12 research groups. Some of them already existed before AWSB was established, others have been newly set up, and bring together expertise from the various research centres. Nearly all groups are interdisciplinary and all groups participate in the AWSB-teaching programme.

A post-graduate teaching programme
The Research School offers doctoral researchers a curriculum of theory, methods and skills required for effective participation in the field of social and economic policy research. An individual practical component, the doctoral research project, is complemented by modular class teaching. This includes both general and specialized compulsory courses and a variety of optional elements. The teaching programme offers far more than the basic requirements for the succesful completion of particular doctoral research projects. Its aim is to prepare the participants for all positions requiring advanced skills in carrying out, managing and evaluating social and economic policy research, be it in the public or the private sector.

Recent developments
The Ministries of Social Affairs and Employment (SZW) and of Public Health, Welfare and Sports (VWS) have showed considerable interest in the AWBS-initiative right from the outset in 1989. Within both departments the need existed for the identification and analysis of a number of long-term developments. SZW, VWS and AWSB reached an agreement on long-term cooperation in 1991.

The board of AWSB aims to stimulate closer coherence between the school's various research programmes. The accumulation of knowledge has also been a major incentive for the Government in terms of support for research schools. Research schools are expected to develop into expert centres in the field of their own research in the Netherlands and thus be able to compete at European level.

To achieve these aims AWSB has been experimenting with various modes of research programming in the past years. The departmental funds played an instrumental role in these experiments. Research which is financed by the two

170

ministries must meet stricter criteria with regard to subject and coherence than research financed by the research centres themselves out of their own budgets. From 1995 onwards the strategy has been to formulate research themes which encompass roughly half of the schools' AIO-projects starting in a particular year. These projects are then matched by departmental grants which are made available for that theme. 1995 saw the start of the programme 'Minimum Protection in the Light of the European Integration', 1996 heralded the programme 'Employment and Social Participation', and in 1997 two programmes started, 'Government and the Market Place' and 'The Future of Social Security'. These programmes will continue in the years thereafter. In 1998 the last two mentioned programmes will be complemented by two more core programmes, 'Citizenship' and 'Pluralism and Equality'.

The cooperation between SZW, VWS and AWSB was externally evaluated in 1995 and all partners agreed to renew their agreement for another four year period. Obviously the financial benefits of this extension are considerable: each department will make available up to Dfl. 500.000 per year. More important though is the continuation of the strategic research alliance between the three partners. This has proven to be of considerable benefit to both the academic community and the policy makers.